What people are saying about *The Future of Knowledge*:

"Our challenge as leaders, executives, and educators is to create organizations that are able to adapt and contribute positively to the environments they serve. In *The Future of Knowledge*, Verna Allee persuasively shows us how the rapid changes in our thinking about organizations and work can contribute to bringing about true and equitable prosperity. She demonstrates that we must add a new cognitive dimension to our economic thinking in order to understand and optimize the new network realities of enterprises and their impact on the entire world."

—John D. Adams, Ph.D.,
Director Organizational Systems Program, Saybrook Graduate School

"*The Future of Knowledge* covers Verna Allee's immense grasp of emerging business realities for all industries. The success of leadership lies within one's capacity to understand the vast white space referred to as the "intangibles" that exist throughout our economy. Through Verna's writing and practice, intangibles become tangible and the invisible becomes visible. Exposure to Allee's models and methodologies will help any practitioner to systematically expose, expand and act upon the domain of value creation for themselves, their organizations and for their customers."

—Charles Armstrong, CEO,
S.A. Armstrong Limited, Canada

"If you want to increase the tangible and intangible assets of your company, rush to Verna Allee's new book. It shows you in a very innovative clear and simple way how it's all working. She gives also very challenging insights on tomorrow's business and society."

—Marc Luyckx Ghisi,
Former member of the Forward Studies Unit of the European Commission, Brussels, (1990–99), Director of "Vision 2020," a think tank on the Paradigm shift.

"Verna Allee has created the next step in providing a framework and a tool to deal with the ever elusive intangibles. It gives hope that the soft side of the organization can be measured!"

—Victor Gulas,
Chief Knowledge Officer of MWH Global, Inc.

"If the modern corporation is to make meaningful progress in the coming century, it has to radically re-orient itself around today's sources of wealth – networked people and knowledge. Verna Allee's latest book makes a serious contribution to helping advance our understanding of the new rules and strategies we must follow to build sustainable high performance in a knowledge-based economy."

—Phil Hood,
CEO Digital 4Sight

"In *The Future of Knowledge* Verna Allee has interwoven complex subjects in an easy to understand way with outstanding lucidity and flow. I recommend this book for executives and managers of every level—in every industry. *The Future of Knowledge* is the future of your business!"

—Bipin Junnarkar,
Vice President Data and Knowledge Management, HP

"Leaders who want to create sustainable businesses must read Allee's book to understand the importance of using organizational order and disorder to create prosperity through networks. This well researched guide helps us understand and learn the new language and tools to create wealth from intangibles."

—Sharon Oriel,
Director, Global Intellectual Capital Tech Center, The Dow Chemical Company

"This book again shows Verna Allee's great gift for making the complex simple and practical. In [*The Future of Knowledge*] she builds and explores the metaphor of enterprise as a living network, successfully weaving together such diverse threads as value network analysis, communities of practice, social network analysis and biology. She shows us what to focus on now and, as always, provides a glimpse of the future. If you want to know what's coming next in this rapidly evolving field, read this book."

—Melissie Rumizen, Ph.D.
author *The Complete Idiot's Guide to Knowledge Management*
and Knowledge Strategist at Buckman Laboratories, Inc.

"Breaking new ground, Verna gives meaning to how the networked organization can be understood at a practical everyday level. She pushes the edge of our collective understanding on how organizations can prosper as they cope with the new business rules imposed by the networks that are emerging to redefine every aspect of business. A fascinating read that will challenge your assumptions about how it all works!"

—Hubert Saint-Onge, CEO,
<konvergeandknow>, former Senior Vice-President, Strategic Capabilities at Clarica

"Understanding intangibles has become one of the most important business and economic questions all over the world. Verna Allee takes us beyond industrial age management practices and shows us that people are the active agents in value creation. Using her revolutionary *HoloMapping*™ techniques she makes "simplexity" out of the complex world of intangibles and people. *The Future of Knowledge* is a book that will have a strong influence on management thinking and education in the years to come."

—Egil Sandvik,
HR Norway and Head of Forum for Intellectual Capital, Norway

"During the 1990s, a plethora of books appeared on Knowledge Management. Many of these books concentrated on how a company could gain a competitive edge in the business world. What these books perhaps overlooked was that today's business world is an entirely different one—it is a world of networked patterns in which social relationships are paramount. Verna Allee's new book is groundbreaking for it asks the only question that matters—What do we need to pay attention to in order to be successful? Knowledge is only one of the capabilities which flow through the interrelated networks of a company, its employees, it suppliers and its clients. *The Future of Knowledge* helps us realize that those in the systemic, interrelated business world now need to pay attention to so much more."

—Kim Sbarcea,
Chief Knowledge Officer, Ernst & Young Australia

"Unless you are able to unlock the mystery of creating value from intangibles, your business is dead. Verna Allee's new book holds one of the keys. The Value Network approach is a powerful and practical method based on theoretically sound principles. A must read."

—Karl-Erik Sveiby,
author, *The New Organizational Wealth*, founder Sveiby Knowledge Management

Praise for *The Knowledge Evolution:*

"This unique book blends the enduring wisdom of the past with the fresh thinking of today in order to provide a remarkably intriguing look into the future of tomorrow's business world."

—Dr. Stephen R. Covey,
author, *Seven Habits of Highly Effective People*

The Future of Knowledge

Increasing Prosperity Through Value Networks

The Future of Knowledge

Increasing Prosperity Through Value Networks

↩

VERNA ALLEE

↩

Amsterdam, Boston, London, New York, Oxford, Paris,
San Diego, San Francisco, Singapore, Sydney, Tokyo

Butterworth-Heinemann is an imprint of Elsevier Science.

Copyright © 2003 Elsevier Science (USA). All rights reserved.

 Recognizing the importance of preserving what has been written, Elsevier Science prints its books on acid-free paper whenever possible.

Library of Congress Cataloging-in-Publication Data

British Library Cataloguing-in-Publication Data
A catalogue record for this book is available from the British Library.

Includes bibliographical references and index.
ISBN: 0-7506-75918 (pbk. : alk. paper)

Artwork©Hermera Technologies Inc. Copyright© 2003 Verna Allee and Associates and its licensors. All rights reserved.

The publisher offers special discounts on bulk orders of this book. For information, please contact:

Manager of Special Sales
Elsevier Science
200 Wheeler Road
Burlington, MA 01803
Tel: 781-313-4700
Fax: 781-313-4882

For information on all Butterworth-Heinemann publications available, contact our World Wide Web home page at: http://www.bh.com

10 9 8 7 6 5 4 3 2 1

Printed in the United States of America

Table of Contents

Preface

Oh, no—not another book on knowledge! There are already so many. At the time I was writing *The Knowledge Evolution* in the summer of 1996, there were only about one hundred articles and fewer than a dozen books in the popular press that were addressing knowledge in organizations. Since then we have seen a flood of hundreds of books, journals, and articles on knowledge and business. Surely we don't need another.

Well, this is a different kind of book. It isn't about knowledge management. It is about how business knowledge *itself* is evolving to an entirely new level. This book shows how we are focusing on knowledge and intangibles as creative questions to prepare ourselves for a very different world of enterprise—one that is fluid, complex, and more interdependent than ever before experienced in human history. Going beyond theory, this book lays out a path forward, builds on new approaches that are working for companies now, and provides previews of newly discovered tools and methods.

THE NETWORK PATTERN OF ORGANIZATIONS

The book begins with a knowledge question: How is business knowledge evolving? What do we need to know for the future as well as for today? What is the pattern of our learning and where are we hoping it will take us?

But before we can answer those questions, we must first understand how organizations are changing. There are many other books that look at business models and "new rules," but they usually look at only one industry or aspect at a time. This book addresses the larger patterns that are unfolding. We know organizational boundaries have been stretched, morphed, and redefined to a degree unimaginable ten years ago. But what is the underlying pattern of the change?

The view expressed here is that businesses are evolving into the networked patterns of living systems. The Internet, which itself expresses the principles of a living network, is allowing the natural network pattern of organizations to emerge.

We have mastered engineering and re-engineering, but living systems require a different mindset and completely different management tools. To develop the skills and knowledge we need for this more comple economy, we are engaged in a business learning journey that extends beyond knowledge management, customer relationship management, e-business, or any one business question. The meta-level learning that we are all engaged in is learning to work with network principles.

The intent of this book is to explore the edges of our learning while offering a practical view of the tools and methods that support new ways of thinking. The chapters are laid out to take people a step at a time through the context of change and the emerging technologies, processes, practices, behaviors, and methods that are supporting business success in the networked world of organizations. Here is a quick overview of what lies ahead.

PART I: THE SHAPE OF THINGS TO COME

Part I sets the context for the practical applications and methods in the chapters that follow. It looks at the business environment and the way organizations, management thinking, and business methods are evolving.

Chapter 1, "Introduction: The Center Keeps Moving," takes a broad look at how business is evolving into network patterns of relationships as knowledge and intangibles forge a new foundation for the economy.

Chapter 2, "A New Prosperity," considers how an economy based on intangibles could provide a better foundation for true wealth and prosperity than one based only on tangible goods.

Chapter 3, "Evolution of Business Thinking," broadly outlines the shifting business and economic assumptions that are leading to new views of the organization, tracing the learning curve along a continuum of knowledge complexity.

Chapter 4, "Living Networks," examines whether organizations have the characteristics of living systems and what we might begin to notice if we view businesses this way.

Chapter 5, "Learning into Complexity," offers suggestions for working with complexity and provides a quick overview of specific practices and tools that are already bringing success at three levels of mastery: the strategic, the tactical, and the operational.

PART II: OPERATIONAL ENTERPRISE KNOWLEDGE

These two chapters discuss some of the practical issues involved with ensuring that people have the knowledge they need to do their everyday tasks.

Chapter 6, "Power and Limits of Technology," explores how the Internet is enabling the natural network pattern of organizations to emerge as new forms of enterprise, networked organizations, business webs, and economic clusters. It also considers the way portals and content are organized and used.

Chapter 7, "The Web of Knowledge," tackles some of the dominant myths around knowledge sharing and replication of best practices, making a case that the real unit of knowledge production is not only the individual but also the collective.

PART III: TACTICAL APPROACHES FOR SENSE MAKING

This section turns the spotlight on the social life of knowledge, exploring the way knowledge emerges in and travels through networks, communities, and webs of conversations.

Chapter 8, "Knowledge Networks and Learning Communities," shows how companies are using communities of practice to support knowledge creation, learning, and competency building. This chapter features a powerful tool that can help make knowledge networks visible and provides a checklist of support for learning communities at different stages of development.

Chapter 9, "Communal Learning and Beyond," assesses how different group learning approaches—from action reviews to conscious conversations—support different modes of learning to improve and apply collective intelligence.

PART IV: NEW STRATEGIC PERSPECTIVES AND TOOLS

Chapter 10, "The New World of Intangibles," introduces intangible assets and indexes, comparing this view of enterprise to that of balanced scorecards and triple–bottom line accounting. The chapter then breaks new ground by proposing a synthesis based on a whole-system approach to value.

Chapter 11, "Intangibles Go to Market," goes beyond intangibles as assets to showcase the different ways that companies can leverage intangibles as negotiable goods and as deliverables. Understanding exchange as the molecular level of economic activity opens new possibilities for understanding value creation.

Chapter 12, "The Value Network Perspective," pulls together the new approaches into a value network perspective, using a case study to demonstrate a powerful mapping methodology that reveals the real value dynamics of any company, business web, or economic cluster.

Chapter 13, "Value Network Examples," features a number of different applications and cases, showing the versatility of the value network perspective.

PART V: PRINCIPLES FOR PROSPERITY

The final section reviews the essential elements for healthy living networks, discussing the implications for how people need to manage themselves, their role, and their relationships for greater prosperity.

Chapter 14, "New business Fundamentals," teases out the essential elements and principles that people need to pay attention to for greater success for themselves and the systems they are part of. It provides a glimpse of the economic future of knowledge as an intangible asset, negotiable, and deliverable that can be leveraged to create value and usher in a new prosperity.

Chapter 15, "Reflections," probes the deep responsibility we hold with our capacity for self-creation and explores what is required to tap a deeper level of collective wisdom.

Using an organic metaphor for organizations is nothing new. Management theorists have been considering organizations as organisms and living systems for several decades. However, most of these explorations have been confined to narrow academic circles or have remained at the level of theory and metaphor. My goal in this work is to build a bridge to everyday business practice by showcasing methods and approaches that are proving to be especially effective for producing business results. These examples and methods demonstrate the skills and capacities that we will need to be successful in a more complex world.

> *The old ways are dissolving and the new has not yet shown itself.*
> *If this is true, then we must engage with one another differently,*
> *as explorers and discoverers.*
>
> Meg Wheatley, *Leadership and the New Science*

Acknowledgments

Writing a book is always an odyssey of discovery, and I have been blessed with the company of many fellow travelers. There are three special people who poked, prodded, and nudged to keep me moving and on track. First there is my editor, Karen Maloney, who masterfully enticed me with just the right degree of challenge and temptation to start me on the journey. While Karen dangled the carrot in front of me, Melissie Rumizen employed a good-humored stick via phone and e-mail from the far corners of the earth. Fran Kelly, a most amazing sister and editor, kept me organized, on schedule, and on target, dishing out love, deadlines, and suggestions in dizzying abundance.

I am also deeply grateful to Juanita Brown, David Isaacs, Rita Cleary, Derek Ransley, Mac Patrick, Al Pozos, Barbara Mayron, Charles Armstrong, and the Digital4Sight group, who early on saw value in this work and encouraged me to keep moving forward. Charles Armstrong, Margaret Logan, and the great team at Konverge and Know, Inc. have helped enormously in making my work accessible with the Web-based *Verna Allee Toolkit*. They also generously contributed several of Leif Frankling's illustrations for this book. A number of knowledge pioneers have provided valuable support as friends and thinking partners: Karl-Erik Sveiby, Elizabeth Reuthe, Sharon Oriel, Karl Wiig, Hubert Saint-Onge, Bipin Junnarkar, RS Moorthy, Baruch Lev, Leif Edvinsson, and Steve Barth. My appreciation of visual facilitation stems from conversations with masters of the craft: David Sibbet, Nancy Margulies, Sherrin Bennet, and Jennifer

Landau. Special thanks go also to Anita Burke, Dinesh Chandra, Sandra Florstedt, Elisabet Sahtouris, Valdis Krebs, and Bernard Lietaeur for their encouragement and suggestions.

PART I

∿

*The Shape of
Things to Come*

ONE

Introduction: The Center Keeps Moving

There is really only one management question: What do we need to pay attention to in order to be successful? One question, but one that has many facets. Business people knew what to pay attention to thirty years ago: profits, expenses, production, and labor. Today the answers, if we can find them at all, have changed enormously and lead to even more questions. Many of the same management words are still around but the surrounding language has evolved and expanded. Some familiar words have totally different nuances today, and we have a whole range of new ones to describe the digital world of business. Almost all our business and managing concepts have expanded, evolved into something else, or been replaced. Many of the old rules for creating value no longer apply. We now must pay attention to different things and learn new questions.

Yet, for the most part, we are still paying attention to the same things we used to, especially when it comes to thinking about organizations. We put our attention on the center and ignore the edges. Our focus isn't really on business in general; it is on companies. The business press is filled with articles that feature a company as the central character in the great drama of business. Stories about companies also focus on the center within that center—the CEO and the leadership team. We have been focused on the parts instead of the whole system.

The corporation has been central to our thinking for a long time, but organizations have become so slippery now. They keep moving, changing, and morphing into other forms. The edges are blurred and fuzzy and seem to be spilling over into other organizations. It is getting harder to tell where one leaves off and another begins. This can be an advantage. Innovation almost always emerges from the in-between places, at the edges. Fuzzy boundaries create innovation spaces where new forms and practices are emerging.

Like a universe expanding, the reach of every company is expanding with the help of the Internet. The center of power is shifting out to the edges. Decisions are moving out from corporate headquarters to individual business units. Business units in turn distribute power and decision making to self-managed teams and profit centers. Production units and team members can be in any corner of the globe. Central control is not only impractical; it is becoming impossible. Instead of mandates passing through chains of command, we find streams of data and information flowing in every direction throughout the organization, so people can make their own decisions and adjust their actions.

How would we describe the world of business if we told the story from the edges, instead of from the center? What would we see if we stopped studying "the organization" or "the company" and focused instead on what is changing and how things are moving between the companies? What patterns and relationships would we see?

We can and are finding ways to shift our viewpoint so we can do just that. We are starting to look at the in-between places and the not-so-visible aspects of business relationships, focusing on knowledge, networks, intangibles, and emotional intelligence.

New Fundamentals Are Emerging

What do we need to pay attention to now? One has only to look at some of the hot management topics to find the learning edge for managers and leaders. Along with many of my colleagues, I have been talking with people from all over the world on these issues. Some of these conversations are with leaders and executives, but many are with middle managers and corporate support groups, including IT, finance, and human resources. They include not only people in companies and corporations but also those in nongovernmental organizations (NGOs), government agencies, and even the military.

We now know we need to pay attention to knowledge. We must understand how to better leverage organizational knowledge and intelligence to create value. The knowledge question has fired the imagination of people in every type of organization and at every level of community and government. It has swept every continent and nation from Canada to Brazil and Venezuela, from Japan and Korea through India and China, Australia, and New Zealand.

We now know that intangibles and intellectual capital need to be treated as true strategic assets. Thinking about intangible assets in business is far more revolutionary than was first apparent. Yet it makes sense that intangibles such as brand image and human competence are vital to success. Corporate citizenship and environmental responsibility are also becoming strategic concerns for companies everywhere. These too are intangible aspects of value that we are learning to pay attention to. Companies and economists struggle to develop new scorecards, metrics, and analytics that will provide leading indicators for how well a company or country is building capability for the future.

We now know that we must learn how to be better global citizens and business people. The diversity movement of the 1990s has expanded to embrace global diversity as we learn to work with and in different cultures around the world. Economic imbalances are being more closely scrutinized, with increasing pressure to seek cross-national policy solutions to trade issues, intellectual property rights, and security. We cannot afford to sit on the sidelines while policies affecting the future of all of us are up for discussion. We must find ways that the knowledge economy can usher in a new era of global prosperity.

We know too that every enterprise must pay attention to how the digital technology evolution is unfolding. E-business and the digital revolution are still "hot" focus areas, even after the bursting of the dot-com bubble. Every type of business has been impacted, and the current technology explosion is far from over.

These new issues that we are paying attention to are helping us learn to live successfully in a more complex world of globally enmeshed organizations. They are creative questions that will lead us to our future. A truly creative question is one that unfolds into new insights and understandings that are so powerful they usher us in to a new worldview and a new identity. They open the pathways we need for expanding our collective consciousness and intelligence to meet the challenges before us.

But how are we to make sense of all this? Hot management topics pop up with head snapping frequency. In a world where everything is important, how do we find what is most important?

A LARGER STORY UNFOLDING

We begin by finding the larger story. The larger story is about the changing nature, structure, and identity of organizations themselves. It isn't about knowledge in organizations or about the digital revolution, although they are certainly aspects of what is happening. More important than either of these, though, is the fact that we are in the midst of a fundamental reinventing of business and economic models. It is about time. Our present accounting methods were developed during the Renaissance, and most of our management practices come from bureaucratic and military models that have dominated management practices for decades.

When we delve into questions of knowledge, intangibles, and true global prosperity, we find our assumptions about business and economics are knocked right off their foundations. Knowledge is an infinite resource that challenges the dominant economic models grounded in scarcity. Viewing intangibles as assets, as negotiable "goods," and as deliverables could potentially make terms like "for profit" and "not-for-profit" obsolete. The old economic order has not been successful in bridging the gap between rich and poor. Traditional business models and structures are cumbersome, costly, and too slow.

We are finally realizing that those old enterprise models and management tools are simply inadequate for the world we are in now. As a whole society, we now need to hone our ability to live and thrive in a world where the adversarial stances between society, business, and political systems no longer make sense. We seek new foundations, new principles, and new tools that support sustainable economic success and bring true prosperity and well-being for all.

The More Things Stay the Same, The More They Change

Are organizations really changing that much? Since Davidow and Malone heralded the arrival of the virtual corporation in 1992,[1] people have predicted the end of the corporation and the rise of the network. However, a quick tour of labor statistics for the past ten years reveals that corporations are still very much alive and well.

The distribution of people employed by firms has held relatively steady since 1992. Far from jumping the corporate ship to become "free agents," roughly the same number of people still collect regular paychecks from a company. People may be changing jobs more often, but they still work for a company. The self-employment rate actually *dropped* about one percent during the same period.[2]

There does not appear to be any large exodus from corporations, despite huge recessionary layoffs at giants such as Motorola and AT&T. There has been a slight dip in the number of people employed by companies with more than 1,000 employees, but the distribution mostly migrated to somewhat smaller companies.

Even the small business employment percentages have remained fairly stable overall, with small firms hovering at around half of the private sector economy. The stability of the number is due to some small firms becoming large firms and some large firms shrinking into small firms.

However, right alongside the relatively stable core of corporate America, the small business sector of the economy is proving to be an increasingly robust engine of growth. Small firms constituted about three-quarters of the employment growth and 90 percent of the new-business location growth during the 1990s.

The ratio of new companies to those going out of business has been showing a steady positive increase, attesting to the vitality of the small business sector. It is these smaller businesses, many without a payroll, that represent most of the growth in the economy.

An analysis by the U.S. Small Business Administration in year 2000 notes that most of the actual growth in employment is from small firms that grow large, while the largest decrease shows up in large business manufacturing.[3] Large firms have stability, but they do not have nearly the degree of growth that small companies enjoy.

A New World of Organizations

So if employee distribution across corporations isn't all that different, are things really changing or not? Yes they are changing—dramatically and fast. The networked economy is not a myth. A critical factor in the growth of a business is a firm's ability to amplify and expand its influence via the Internet and digital technologies. Small businesses actively and deliberately enlarge their business networks, entering into strategic alliances that help expand their brands, strengthen capability, and help distribute products globally.

The Internet allows even the smallest of companies to have a global presence and contract for work anywhere in the world. People can now easily find each other and organize themselves to achieve all manner of goals. There is a variety of digitally enabled business networks for marketing, locating materials and resources, and expanding distribution, all providing value for their participants.

There are also social networks, political networks, professional networks, and networks for communities and enthusiasts—all purposeful, all providing value for their participants. Ad hoc watchdog organizations band together on the Internet, acting as a vocal counterbalance to corporate and government excesses. People join together in networks in the interest of social service, from supporting education of the public about cancer to tackling complex social issues such as corruption, poverty, and human rights abuses.

The center *is* moving. It is moving out from corporate hubs to more diffuse and distributed webs of business relationships and alliances spreading across the globe.

COMPANIES BEHAVING LIKE BUSINESS WEBS

The corporation itself is often organizing more like a business network than a traditional company. Workers who used to be tucked snug inside corporate walls are roaming the roads and working from home. They are increasingly world travelers, even if only by videoconference. Project team members can be scattered all over the planet, collaborating and working together without ever meeting face to face.

Business relationships are changing even inside a company. Business units and service groups may bid for projects and compete directly with outside suppliers to provide services to their own company. One finds businesses within businesses within larger businesses within business webs. Hierarchies become irrelevant, unnecessary, and frequently just a darned nuisance.

The steady increase in telework is contributing to the business web environment. According to the International Telework Association and Council, in 2001 approximately 28 million, or one in five U.S. employees participated in some form of teleworking. This is a 17 percent increase over year 2000. Economic advantage is the primary driver. IBM cites $100 million in savings annually from telecommuting and mobile work. By 2004, it is expected that 35 percent of enterprises will systematically re-evaluate job locations, moving the work to where it makes the most business and economic sense.[4]

Money Moves Differently

The moving center of business means the money moves differently too. Digital transactions have changed the nature of banking and finance. Commerce flows freely between states and nations over the Internet, and vendors often set up their businesses where they can conveniently sidestep sales taxes, business taxes, and even zoning laws. Complementary currencies such as flyer award miles are shifting some economic transactions away from the bank-controlled monetary system.

Everybody is learning the art of the contract as more people work on a project basis. This is quite challenging for tax services and the Internal Revenue Service is directly addressing the situation. It has been issuing new guidelines for business deductions for home office expenses and independent contractor status. State sales tax laws are being revised to address interstate or international sales over the Internet.

Income reporting requirements sometimes get in the way of business model innovations. Groups of people who want to act as a business network and contract for projects or work together, are often squeezed into corporate legal structures that don't fit their business models. The limited liability corporation (LLC) business model is growing in usage, but it cannot solve all the issues that arise. For example, some employees are negotiating for more participation in corporate profits from their innovations. The money issues keep popping up, corporate boundaries keep moving, and the agencies and policy makers scramble to catch up.

RECONFIGURING BUSINESS RELATIONSHIPS

The nature of outsourcing and partnering relationships is changing so much that the center can be anywhere. Outsourcing and alliances are being used to drive enterprise transformation. Whether the goal is dramatic growth, market repositioning, or rapid diversification, outsourcing and partnering are expanding from the cost savings side toward strategic growth.

Outsourcing Redefines Relationships

Large corporations are outsourcing everything from IT and logistics to decorative plant services and corporate art exhibits. Worldwide spending on outsourcing services in 1999 totaled $116 billion.

This trend is not confined to private industry. Government agencies are aggressively using outsourcing to reinvent government, on both sides of the Atlantic. In the U.K., Inland Revenue (counterpart to the U.S. Internal Revenue Service) has outsourced its entire IT function, selling its assets and transferring more than 2,000 employees to a partner organization. The Belgian Post has entered a joint venture with a consulting firm. In the U.S., NASA has outsourced most of its computer hardware support. One of the top priorities of the Bush Administration is to use more public-private companies for federal work. The 2000 Fair Act inventory shows that nearly half of the 1.7 million civilian jobs in the federal government could eventually be outsourced.[5]

Greater Interdependency

More important than the numbers is the nature of the relationships. Outsourcing decisions used to be driven by spinning off *noncritical* business processes and functions. Now it may be strategically advantageous to outsource *core* processes in order to bring them quickly up to competitive readiness. This could mean that even core processes are moving away from the center.

In 2001, the Accenture Institute for Strategic Change conducted interviews with 26 large firms in the U.S., Europe, and Asia. They found that 31 percent are partnering to dramatically improve business capabilities that are critical to the firm's success.[6]

This type of deeply interdependent relationship requires finding a real business ally, not just a vendor. The degree of strategic coupling between the participants moves beyond value chain dynamics with its plug-and-play vendors to value network dynamics, where participants engage more as equals and develop deeper relationships. Even for core business processes, the center can be anywhere.

NETWORKED ENTERPRISE MODELS

The Internet makes the work of integrating multiple partners nearly seamless. It also reduces the cost of transactions of every type. Digital technologies are starting to pay off, demonstrated by big productivity gains starting in 2001.[7] Traditionally, one of the driving factors in company formation has been to reduce transaction costs by efficiencies of scale, both vertical and horizontal. The Internet has made that far less of a factor. John Hagel, well-known author and consultant in the Internet revolution, calls for breaking corporations into their essential elements, in what he dubs the "molecular" organization.[8] In his view, most organizations are an "unnatural bundle" of three very different businesses: finding and building customer relationships; creating products; and managing infrastructure. He suggests companies pick one and rely on others for the other two.

Companies are already doing just that. Dell Computer and Nike led the way in extensive partnering. Following suit, about 70 percent of Cisco's hardware products going to customers are shipped directly from its deeply interconnected partners who make the products. A Cisco employee never has to actually handle the goods. Amazon.com has only 7,800 employees, but it aggregates and sells enormous volumes of merchandise from thousands of vendors (over $3 billion in 2001) through an innovative web of relationships, with very little warehousing.[9] Anyone can become an Amazon associate and offer books and merchandise through their own personal or business Web site, collecting a small commission along the way. Therefore, looking at employee profiles for large companies can be deceiving. The size of a company's value network can be much larger than it would appear at first glance.

These complex relationships have given rise to what the Digital4Sight group refers to as business webs or b-webs. Business webs are partner networks of producers, service providers, suppliers, infrastructure companies, and customers linked via digital channels. In the late 1990s, the group conducted an extensive two-year research study focusing on evolving business models and digital enterprise.[10] They found that innovative companies such as eBay and Cisco were developing new ways to create and deliver value through both human and digital networks. Through extensive use of Internet technologies, Cisco broke the rules on knowledge sharing and changed the playing field for its industry.

The study demonstrates that a number of business models such as markets, alliances, and distributive networks are now much easier to assemble and manage, sparking increasing innovation in business models. Even classic business models such as aggregators who sell goods from multiple sources and value chains might involve extensive networks of resource partners yet manage them easily with digital technologies.[11]

Redefining the Organization

The concept of the organization emerged at a time when most businesses were bureaucracies designed around strict hierarchies. The human boundary of the organization was, and still is, largely determined on the basis of who is an employee or a member. If you are an employee, you are inside; if you aren't, you are outside. That worked for awhile, because large companies, in terms of financial transactions and revenue, also had large numbers of employees. Today revenue and employee numbers don't match up as neatly, as shown by the populations of members participating in AOL and Amazon that contribute content or referrals. Today a company with relatively few actual employees can have a value network that includes tens of thousand of suppliers, millions of members, and billions of dollars in revenue.

Given the developments of the last decade, it is time to rethink what we mean by an organization and begin to use the term more in its biological sense. *Webster's Universal Encyclopedic Dictionary* defines the organization as "an administrative and functional structure. However, this now feels too narrow and rigid. *The American Heritage Dictionary* simply defines the organization as "a structure through which individuals cooperate systematically to conduct business." However, this dictionary also suggests a more basic definition that gets a little closer to the way we are starting to view business activities: "Something made up of elements with varied functions that contribute to the whole and to collective functions: an organism." This more organic definition opens the possibility that we may learn to work with companies as truly "living entities."

Today I would define an organization as "a complex adaptive social system where people systematically cooperate to achieve a common purpose." This definition puts the social system first instead of the structure. Organizational structure cannot exist without a social system that creates and supports it. We will take a closer look at the advantages of putting people first in the following chapters.

Steep Learning Curves

The new networked world of organizations is all about relationships, but the corporate track record for building successful business alliances is pitiful. For example, an Accenture study across all industries, reported in 2002, found that for every 100 alliance negotiations, 90 fail to reach agreements and only two survive more than four years. More than half of those that do manage to survive fall well short of expectations.[12] That is a dismally high failure rate given the growing importance of being able to build good business relationships.

Most of the business literature on webs and value networks overlooks the new business ethics that are needed for success in a world of complex business relationships and interdependencies. Some companies, such as Cisco, have had a strong culture of partnering and collaboration since the launch of the company. Other technology companies, however, are still operating with the old competitive, rapacious mindset. Companies such as Oracle and Microsoft, founded with different cultures, find themselves struggling to build the same quality of relationships throughout their own business webs.

The foundation of good business relationships has been and always will be trust. Character counts. There is a new ethical underpinning for success that requires higher levels of integrity and honesty than have ever before been required. Networks and webs are more transparent than companies, and even companies are more transparent than they were before. Relationships and linkages are visible to everyone. Business deals play out on an increasingly public stage. Corporate ethics can be laid bare in an instant, and beware the company that plays fast and loose with questionable dealings or practices.

Managing From the Edge

The center is not just moving, it is also an illusion. We need to learn to stop looking for the one focal point, the one leader, or the one answer and start sensing patterns. It is not the pieces and parts that are most important. Dynamic relationships and interdependencies are what we must learn to work with, understand, and "manage" from a whole new sense of what that means.

Perhaps what we really need is to manage less and *attend* more. The word "attend" has a range of meanings that are far more appropriate for leaders and managers in the current socioeconomic environment: "to pay attention to, to look after, to be present with, to apply oneself, to apply one's mind and direct one's attention." What do we need to *attend* to in order to be successful and create a more hopeful future?

How Business Knowledge Is Unfolding

We are currently engaged in a global learning journey that is so massive it is altering the perspectives, goals, and behaviors of entire societies. We are forging new relationships, new strategies, identities, purposes, language, and new organizational forms.

As business people, our core learning challenge is to understand network principles and apply them all across our business practices, from technology networks, to human networks, to business networks. Networks constitute the pattern of organization for living systems, which are far too complex to control or engineer. This means learning new tools and methods that will help us see network patterns and work with what is emerging.

1. Operationally, we must understand how digital networks and technologies support people in creating, organizing, and accessing the everyday knowledge they need to complete their tasks and make good decisions.

2. Tactically, we need to understand how social webs such as knowledge networks and communities of practice help create, diffuse, and leverage knowledge and innovation.

3. Strategically, we need to understand our organizations as participants in multiple business networks where intangibles are important for building relationships and smoothing interactions.

4. Everyone, especially leaders, needs to learn the new ethical underpinnings of success for networked organizations, and how to engage with each other in the conversations that matter.

These are the areas where we most need to expand our capacities and intelligence, both individually and collectively. The questions we are asking signal the evolution of management thinking, from the ability to handle things that are complicated to working with those that are truly complex. It is the meta-shift from engineering skills to those that will help us thrive in the more organic world of living networks. In every area we are developing new tools, new practices, and new ways of thinking to support the living webs of business, of the economy, of society, and of the earth in ways that all can thrive. This is the future of knowledge.

Chapter Endnotes

[1] William H. Davidow, and Michael S Malone, *The Virtual Corporation: Structuring and Revitalizing the Corporation for the 21st Century*, Harper Business, 1992.

[2] U.S. Census Bureau, *Employment Size of Firms Statistics*, 1999.

[3] U.S. Small Business Administration. *Small Business Economic Indicators 2000*, Office of Advocacy, 2001.

[4] French Caldwell, "Creating Resiliency with the E-Workplace," Gartner, Inc., January, 3, 2002.

[5] Jane Linder, Alvin Jacobsen, Matthew D. Breitfelder, and Mark Arnold, "Business Transformation Outsourcing: Partnering for Radical Change," Accenture Institute for Strategic Change, July 18, 2001.

[6] Jane Linder, Alvin Jacobsen, Matthew D. Breitfelder, and Mark Arnold, "Business Transformation Outsourcing: Partnering for Radical Change," Accenture Institute for Strategic Change, July 18, 2001.

[7] Anna Bernasek, "The Productivity Miracle Is For Real," *Fortune*, March 18, 2002.

[8] David Kirkpatrick, "Great Leap Forward: From Davos, Talk of Death," *Fortune*, March 5, 2001.

[9] Amazon.com, March 2002. www.amazon.com.

[10] Don Tapscott, David Ticoll, and Alex Lowy, *Digital Capital: Harnessing the Power of Business Webs*, Harvard Business School Press, 2000. The author was involved in this study as a senior analyst, and the *ValueNet Works*™ analysis method, demonstrated in Chapter 12, was one of the analysis tools used for the project.

[11] Don Tapscott, David Ticoll, and Alex Lowy, *Digital Capital: Harnessing the Power of Business Webs*.

[12] Accenture.com, "Grasping the Capability: Successful Alliance Creation and Governance Through the Connected Corporation: Executive Summary," as of March 11, 2002. www.accenture.com.

© 2002 Hemera Technologies Inc.

I spent a long time trying to find my center,
until I looked closely one night and found it had wheels
and moved easily in the slightest breeze,
so now I spend less time sitting and more time sailing.

—Brian Andreas, Artist

TWO

A New Prosperity

The emerging knowledge economy and networked world of enterprise have the potential for dramatically increasing economic and social prosperity in a much different way than we have experienced in the past. As we develop new tools for understanding business in a more systemic, interconnected way, we are ushering in new possibilities for creating our future.

A new urgency to address global prosperity began to surface after the September 11, 2001 attacks on the World Trade Center in New York City. At the World Economic Forum in Davos in early 2001, prior to the attacks, the focus was on the ways business webs or value networks are connecting molecular or modular corporations. At that time, even after the decline of the dot-com frenzy, the focus was all on business and the digital economy. Speakers were trumpeting the end of the corporation and the rise of the network. But the undercurrents were business and economics as usual.

At the early 2002 meeting held in New York in the wake of the attacks, the focus of the Forum was quite different. A somber and serious group of presenters reflected on corporate citizenship and the challenge of addressing world economic imbalances.

The two issues of corporate change and global prosperity are, of course, very related. If unbundled and networked corporations are parceling out parts of their business to whatever company can best fulfill a particular function regardless of geographic location, then that opens the way for technology, service, and manufacturing jobs to be more globally distributed. Digital technologies have enabled many functions to go where the workers are, opening up possibilities for new business and economic models. This trend has not escaped the notice of analysts and business commentators.

However, it is a mistake to think this shift is just about business. It is not.

True Wealth

Even before world attention became focused on the militant extremism that thrives in desperately poor regions of the world, there was a social movement well underway challenging the dominant economic assumptions. That movement has intensified into an insistence that countries frame wealth not just in economic terms, but also in the sense of social health and well-being and healthy ecosystems.

A recent journey pulled together a number of themes for me, leading to a new vision and hope that inspires much of my work in knowledge networks and value creation. The circumstances of my life had not included a great deal of international travel until recent years. Not too long ago, I visited India for the first time, conducting workshops on knowledge and value creation issues in several different cities. Because one of my topics areas was intangible assets, I was especially attuned to questions of wealth.

What struck me in India is not how many people fall through the economic cracks, but how many don't. Half the population of Mumbai lives on the street. The poorest of areas, with people living in makeshift shelters, are intermingled with some of the most prosperous business and residential neighborhoods. In the United States, if you are homeless you are truly among the most destitute people in the population. In India that is not the case at all. Life is hard on the streets, but not all people are destitute. On their tiny patch of footpath in a makeshift shelter, they raise their children, go to their jobs by day, cook and sleep at night, and live a simple existence.

One day while out walking, the friend I was with nodded hello to a street dweller and reminisced with me about when the woman's children were born, although they are all grown now and gone away. The woman's husband had a pushcart business and left every morning to go sell his goods. They had lived in that spot on the street for over eighteen years.

I do not hold a romantic view of this. There is no escaping the hardships of such a life and the difficulties much of the population suffers on a daily basis. Yet, as we walked and drove through the vibrant streets of Mumbai, despite the heartbreak and suffering, I was struck by the vitality and life pulse of this country of so many people. An incredibly diverse economy with more than 1 billion people and 700 different languages somehow works. How is this possible? What keeps it together?

Ordinary conversations hold the clue. In the United States and Europe the next question after "Where are you from?" is always, "What do you do?" meaning what work do you do? The response to that question tells us a great deal about that person's education, upbringing, social status, and economic position.

In India, that second question is "Do you have family?" The question is followed by careful inquiry into the health of your parents, the number of brothers and sisters you have, and where all of you live in relation to each other. People were shocked and sad that my parents live alone several states away from me. I would explain that in America it is a matter of pride for parents not to depend on their children for help, but I could feel their confusion at my response.

I fully understood when one of my new friends looked at me sadly and said very sincerely, "Oh, America is such a poor country—you don't have family." There it was; family is wealth. The true wealth of India is its amazing social fabric. Family ties and connections are so critical to the economy that if you have family you are economically secure. If you have family you have wealth; without it you are destitute. There, the social web of friends and family is the glue that holds life together. It is a tremendous national asset, a great national wealth.

Yet, a strong social infrastructure would never show up as an asset on the national accounts or in economic indicators. Healthy social systems and ecosystems are not economically treated as assets, nor are they regarded as assets in their own right.

These were not new ideas to me, as they are constant themes that underscore my work. But in India a powerful sense of unfairness swept over me that so much that is beautiful and life affirming is never acknowledged in economics or business. We know our economic practices do not serve most of the world's population and are leading to a continuing cycle of environmental degradation. What is it that keeps us repeating the same business practices?

Redefining Wealth and Prosperity

Finding a way to create true prosperity requires that we redefine our terms and reframe our questions. We must penetrate to the very heart of our assumptions about wealth. Bernard Lietaer, expert on global currencies and author of *The Future of Money*, reminds us that the word *wealth* stems from *weal*, implying a condition or state of well-being. In that sense, he defines wealth as "unbounded potential value that can be expressed as material wealth, relationship wealth, a wealth of joy, of love, of culture, of wit, of beauty, of imagination."[1] This type of wealth is expressed in tangible economic terms and also in terms of intangible assets, such as health, education, and security.

We are seeing evidence of a shift toward a broader definition of success in business also, with intangible assets now receiving serious attention. Intangible success indicators are showing up in corporate annual reports. Accountants, economists, national leaders, CFOs, and executive teams are grappling with new management practices that support increasing intangible assets and generating intangible value.

Related to the word *wealth* is *prosperity*, which resonates with many of the themes expressed in this book. One of my favorite definitions of prosperity is as "good fortune." Good fortune has an interesting meaning. Good fortune is not an accident; that would be called "luck." Good fortune does not come about as a result of planning; that is called "good management." If you have good fortune, you are paying very close attention to what is emerging and are working with those forces in order to prosper. So one could say good fortune results from "good sense(ing)." More important than good managing is developing the quality of sensing and paying attention in ways that bring about good fortune in a complex environment.

Prosperity also is a word that is linked to economic growth. It evokes a mental image of something that is thriving and flourishing. The past theory of prosperity and business was the "trickle down" theory. It was reasoned, mostly by the conservative establishment, that if corporations were successful their economic success would eventually "trickle down" through the economy and benefit every social class, including the poor. Trickle down has largely been dismissed by economists for the simple reason that it just doesn't work that way. If the rich get richer then, well, the rich get richer. It does not necessarily follow that other economic classes will ever see any financial benefit for themselves. In fact, what we see more often is a reinforcing loop with the rich becoming richer and the poor becoming even poorer.

Trickle down implies that those on the bottom are dependent on those at the top of the economic order. This mindset permeates the world debate as to whether the rich should be responsible for improving the lot of the poor, entrenching the polarity between social classes and between rich and poor nations. It is also a scarcity model of wealth. Applying this model in the traditional developmental approach to economic disparity is proving to be an abysmal failure. Large-scale development programs often destroy the local economic base and create even greater dependency on the largesse of the wealthier nations.

Increasing Prosperity

The new economy offers an opportunity to radically rethink how prosperity might increase. For one thing, intangible assets are a better foundation for creating true prosperity than are physical materials. The nature of intangibles is such that you can give them away, trade them, or sell them, yet you still have them to use again another day. That doesn't happen with physical resources, which when used up are gone.

In addition, intangibles enjoy a multiplier effect. When people exchange knowledge, they can actually create more knowledge between them. This would never happen with barrels of oil. No wonder economists are scratching their heads. Economist Brian Arthur's revolutionary law of increasing returns is just a sneak preview of what lies ahead once we really begin to understand the dynamics of intangibles![2]

The multiplier effect of knowledge and intangibles, coupled with the way the Internet empowers individuals and small businesses, opens the door of possibilities to a new level of prosperity. Knowledge and intangibles are easy to increase, requiring relatively few natural resources. Expanding an intangible economic resource such as knowledge does not require heavy investment in plants, buildings, land, or machinery.

Knowledge isn't free, however. It requires the right environment for learning as well as access to education and to a digital infrastructure that can support knowledge-intensive business. Computers and communication technology are relatively small investments for a community. As wireless technology develops, we can anticipate whole countries leapfrogging ahead of their weak infrastructure, as third-world businesses dive directly into the world marketplace as suppliers. The rise of India's computer industry provides a glimpse of what we can anticipate seeing on a much larger scale with decreasing costs for wireless and computer technology.

With knowledge, the means of production is shifting from the large, vertically integrated corporation to much smaller groups. Small companies and even individuals can employ digital technologies to connect and work together, moving control of many projects from large corporations to small ones.

One System of Economic and Social Value

The current economic environment drives corporations, governments, and nongovernmental organizations (NGOs) into adversarial relationships. Corporations are expected to be socially responsible citizens and are increasingly brought to task by public opinion for trampling on communities, abusing power and privilege, supporting exploitive trade laws, or sullying the environment. Businesses challenge government agencies to be more supportive of their needs. NGOs beg corporations and foundations for grants to support the social good they would do.

This adversarial stance would largely disappear if, instead of seeing three sectors, we shift our perspective to that of one socioeconomic system generating both tangible and intangible value. Three of my friends, Dinesh Chandra, Prasad Kaipa, and Anil Sachdev, created a Foundation for Human and Economic Development focused on exploring such a perspective. They held a gathering in Lonavala, India that included high-level business people, CEOs, and leaders from both large and small social service and educational groups.

On the first day of the gathering, the conversation revealed two distinct camps. In one group were the education and social services groups with hands outstretched saying to the corporate people, in essence, "Help us, help us, help us." In the other group were the business people who basically were responding, "Why should we?" They were not without compassion, but they had to answer for profits and there was no business benefit that they could see.

That evening my friends set up a group role-playing session to explore this polarity with the group. The rule was that everyone must state their positions and then go to one side of the room or the other. As people made their choices, the gulf grew wider and wider. The atmosphere grew increasingly despairing as the gap seemed so impossible to bridge. A few brave souls declared it was not one or the other that was right; we needed to balance the needs of both. They went to sit in the center. The edges began to curve as people instinctively wanted to come together in a circle.

I held back, watching. There were only a few of us left who had not taken a stand. By this time, there was a large circle of people with two or three in the center. I was concerned that what I would do next might be socially incorrect and I began pacing around the circle a bit nervously.

Finally I spoke out. "I can't do it. I can't play," I said. "I cannot come into the circle, because I don't understand the game. You have set it up as a polarity and I don't understand either wealth or business that way. Balance is the wrong answer, because that still holds the same polarity. Beyond the polarity, I see only one system of value creation where both tangible and intangible value is exchanged. There is just one ecosystem of social and economic value exchanges, and one cannot be separated from the other!" Then I sat down. There was a stunned silence for a minute or so. Then one by one, the remaining people took the same stand and stayed outside the circle also. The next day the whole tone of the conversation was different. People were more thoughtful, genuinely looking for ways they could find common ground and support each other. They had reframed their questions.

FROM SCARCITY TO PROSPERITY

Scarcity and debt creation underpin the current economic system, largely because of the way the monetary system works. However, if we understand monetary value as just one of several kinds of value that are exchanged in society, the world of value looks very different. An economic view based only on money short-changes all the other forms of wealth. When you ask people what they are most grateful for, they rarely list money first. Intangibles such as the support of community, the love of our families, our education, our health, our talents—are our real assets, our true wealth.

We have expressed a need for systems thinking for several years now, but in business we don't typically address the whole system. We still speak of success only in monetary and tangible terms. It is time to move to a fresh perspective. In Chapters 10 through 13 we will explore a way to think about value from a living systems perspective that makes visible the important contributions of intangibles such as knowledge and benefits.

Even as recently as five years ago we were not ready to think about value differently from the way we had for decades. Now we are reaching a critical level of understanding in the business community—of key concerns, concepts, and ideas that will move us forward into this dynamic world of value networks. We are beginning to build a new vocabulary that allows a different kind of conversation to happen. The next two chapters follow the development of this new language that is laying a foundation for thinking about business differently. We *are* ready and we *can* find a better way.

Chapter Endnotes

[1] Bernard Lietaer, *The Future of Money: Creating New Wealth, Work and a Wiser World* (London: Century, 2001).

[2] Brian Arthur, "Increasing Returns and the New World of Business," *Harvard Business Review*, July/Aug 1996.

© 2002 Hemera Technologies Inc.

Finding a way to create true prosperity requires that we redefine our terms and reframe our questions. We must penetrate to the very heart of our assumptions about wealth.

THREE
Evolution of Business Thinking

We are in the midst of two important knowledge evolutions in business. The first is an evolution in how we *think* about business and organizations. The second is how that shift of thinking plays out in *practice*, in the way we work. The two evolutions are happening in symbiotic relationship, and people cannot effectively adopt the new practices without first understanding the emerging assumptions that are shaping our actions.

We will first look inward to explore how our ideas are evolving. In Chapters 4 and 5, I will suggest a way to frame the creative questions we have posed for ourselves. The following chapters will then delve into some of the most promising ideas and practices.

THE EROSION OF CENTRALIZED CONTROL

Every economic change brings new organizational structures and complementary new social structures to support them. Managerial focus also shifts.

Early industrial era

In the early industrial age, strategic resources were raw materials and production facilities. The social structure required to support the economy was pretty straightforward. Labor consisted literally of hired "hands," and people were more or less interchangeable to accomplish simple routine tasks. The easiest way to organize was to devise bureaucratic, hierarchical structures adopted from military models. The goal of managers was to keep things well ordered and under control through careful planning, clear lines of authority, and rules that were incorporated into policies and procedures (see Figure 3.1).

Industrial Era

Later, financial capital began to be more of a foundation, although clearly labor and materials were still important. Financial capital funded expansion and technology advances that led to more sophisticated products and services. As technology became more available,

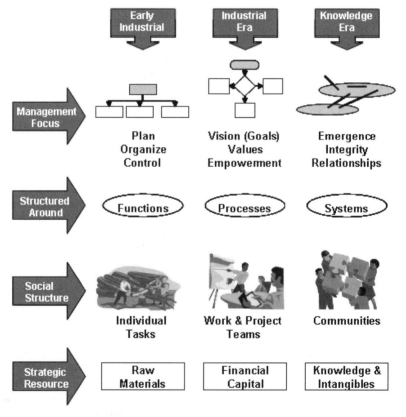

FIGURE 3.1 *Evolution of the organization from the early industrial age to the present.*

companies achieved competitive advantage through better processes and quality. Faster time to market could gain early adopter advantage.

It made more sense to organize around processes, which led to fewer levels of bureaucracy and began to flatten the hierarchy. As a result, management tasks and decisions moved outward from corporate executives to business units and workgroups. With the loosening bonds of centralized control, it became important to engage empowered teams through clear vision, goals, and values rather than rigid roles, rules, and policies. That ushered in a work environment employing more humanistic management approaches.

The Total Quality approach brought in new business language and structures that emphasized processes and teams, further distributing decision making out toward smaller and smaller work groups. Today, a team-and-process focus is still the dominant approach for managing organizations.

The Knowledge Economy

We are now in the midst of another shift that is taking decision making and control even further from the center. With digital connectivity and increasing access to information, the primary resource for competitive advantage is shifting from financial capital to knowledge and information. This has also led to a shift in social structure, as control of the work has moved to smaller and smaller units. We are rapidly moving toward a time when individuals control their own means of production and manage their own inputs, outputs, commitments, contracts, and profitability. This is true whether they are working within the boundaries of a corporation or externally as a sole proprietorship or contract worker.

When decision making is thus distributed, planning and organizing in traditional ways no longer works. There are simply too many variables. As a result, managerial focus is moving toward a more participative rather than controlling stance. Like those who practice good fortune, leaders must sense what is emerging and work with it. When there are so many variables and players involved, the new strategic focus is placed on building relationships across the value network and fostering knowledge-sharing communities.

Even though the overall progression in business focus is moving toward knowledge, intangibles, communities, and relationships, many businesses are still organized in more traditional ways. In many cases this is quite appropriate. But more often these ways no longer work that well; simple inertia is keeping the old structures in place.

An Underlying Shift of Worldview

The current focus on the less visible aspects of business and organizations is one more expression of a major evolution of ideas about how the world works. Our business questions are aspects of the deep societal shift from the Cartesian mechanistic worldview based on Newtonian physics, to a more dynamic, interconnected view drawing insights from quantum physics, complexity theory, behavioral science, social theory, and living systems. This knowledge evolution has been happening since the power of the quantum world of physics was demonstrated so horrifically in World War II. However, this shift of worldview was accelerated by a defining moment.

In the late 1960s, human society experienced a powerful shift of human consciousness when we first saw the breathtaking images of the earth from outer space. We discovered that national borders are not visible from space—only land masses, brilliant blue seas, and ephemeral swirls of drifting clouds. Suddenly an identity dependent on national borders and man-made barriers seemed arbitrary and confining.

Soon after, the Berlin Wall came tumbling down. People, faxes, and e-mail messages began flowing freely across national boundaries. Information connectivity began firing the electronic synapses of a collective global intelligence that was gradually becoming aware of itself.

That image of the earth also brought a larger awareness of the majesty and fragility of the complex global ecosystem that supports all of us. Satellite imagery brought shocking evidence of how seriously humans are impacting the global environment by laying waste vast tracts of forest, polluting rivers, and spewing layers of dirty air. We see clear evidence of how human activity can affect global weather systems and seriously impact the health of humans and forests alike. Millions of people are facing increasing difficulty in finding clean water to drink or fertile soil and pastures for their fields, flocks, and herds.

Slowly, many would say too slowly, we are learning a new humility. We are beginning to redefine ourselves not as masters of the universe but as global citizens sailing a precious blue planet through the cosmos together. This deeper awareness of interdependence is constantly reinforced in visits with friends around the world via e-mail and Internet chat rooms. Our common humanity is experienced through media images, such as the peaceful, multicultural kaleidoscope of celebrations as the century turned, contrasted with the faces of suffering in war-torn villages.

Many people now hold a sense of personal identity that includes being a global citizen. There is a growing population of "cultural creatives," those who care deeply about ecology and saving the planet, about relationships, peace, and social justice. They pursue self-actualization, spirituality, and self-expression. As a group they are both inner directed and socially concerned. It has been estimated that there are roughly 50 million people in the United States and 80 to 90 million people in the European Union who would fall into this category as of year 2000.[1] More important, they tend to be vocal and proactive in working for change, believing that a few dedicated individuals can make a difference.

This larger societal awareness is also affecting the way we think about business and economics. Management practices reflect the currents of thought in larger social movements. People in business are now struggling to translate these more human- and earth-centered values into business and economic practice. As a result, current business questions are focusing on complex and systemic aspects of business. Business journals today lean heavily toward topics concerning the unseen, the invisible, and the complex. Lead articles may address knowledge, intangibles, values, ethics, transparency and governance, complexity, sustainability, and even emotional intelligence and spirituality in the workplace.

A Progression of Management Thinking

My book, *The Knowledge Evolution*, introduced seven modes of knowledge and learning ranging along a continuum of increasing complexity. This continuum follows an archetypal pattern that surfaces time and again in theories of intelligence and organizations. (See the Appendix for more on the knowledge complexity archetype.) In that earlier book, I suggested that management science is tracing this continuum as a learning curve for addressing increasingly complex questions.[2] The evolving field of management thinking appears to support that hypothesis.

Two major breakthroughs in modern management preceded the twentieth century. The first of these was the rise of modern accounting during the Renaissance. The invention of the financial "bottom line" has driven business focus and decision making for the past five centuries. The second breakthrough was that of the industrial revolution, bringing the machine metaphor that dominated management thinking from the late 1700s until about 1930. The machine metaphor still permeates management thinking, with a continuing emphasis on "engineering" in both management language and methods.

However, Figure 3.2 shows that the pace of learning gradually picked up after the 1930s, accelerated after 1970, and seems to be continuing at an intense pace. Now we are fascinated with networks, systems, and complexity. We are beginning to view organizations as living systems. Note that with many of these focus areas, pioneers in a field may appear a decade—or even several decades—before a topic shows up on the radar screen of the general business community.

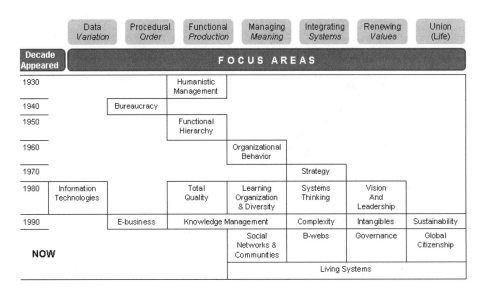

FIGURE 3.2 *Evolution of management thinking. Decade Appeared indicates the time when a focus area appeared in mainstream management thinking.*

THE EXPANDING FOCUS OF THE ENTERPRISE

As the economy has become more complex, the number of things managers must think about has also expanded (see Figure 3.3). In the days of guilds and crafts, workgroups were tightly organized with simple relationships. With the shift to the industrial economy the focus moved to production lines and then to processes. We found that functional units and project teams worked quite well for managing processes. Sometimes different groups work at cross purposes, and there are fiefdoms and turf wars, but nothing so worrisome that a little more engineering wouldn't fix it—or so we thought.

Then we discovered those really big, core business processes that cut across the whole enterprise. So our next challenge was learning to work in cross-functional teams. Of course, if you follow the thread of those processes a bit further, you find they include customer processes and

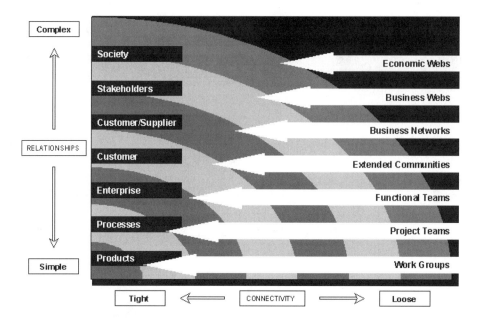

FIGURE 3.3   *Expanding focus of business.³*

even supplier processes. Hmmm, that is starting to get a bit complicated. Then too, there are all those other stakeholders to consider in the extended business webs and economic webs.

Now we are in a bit of trouble. We finally learned how to think in terms of processes instead of functional units, and now we are supposed to understand how to work with webs and networks? Yes, but there is a problem. Networks and webs can't be understood using the same old process tools. We will have to find other approaches, regardless of all those massive investments in enterprise resource planning (ERP) software and SAP. Those systems are often just a frantic effort to stretch the process view far enough to handle complexity.

However, the process view has been stretched to its limits. It won't help us understand networks and complex systems. We will have to think about things differently and find new tools for this next order of complexity.

THE MAGNITUDE OF THE SHIFT

This shift in managerial thinking in the 1990s has been of much greater magnitude than anything seen in business since the industrial revolution. It is large enough to qualify as a true paradigm shift, described by Thomas Kuhn as a radical departure from the accepted way of doing things that founds a new tradition.[4] Knowledge theorist Max Boisot and others suggest that the shift to an information-based economy is driving a species-level evolution equivalent to the development of agriculture and the dawn of the industrial age.[5]

But this shift of worldview is not without difficulty. Many people haven't caught on to how big this is. Whenever a truly new and different body of thought arises, a peculiar social dynamic begins to take place. In its early, formative stages a radically different theory or approach appears as a deviation, perhaps even a depravity or illness. When this happens the social system tries to (1) neutralize it by downgrading its status, (2) attack it outright, or (3) incorporate it into existing schemes. Those of us who have been working with the new

---

Old Paradigm, New Paradigm?

There is a common misconception that a shift from one way of thinking to another is cleaner and simpler than it actually is. There is no neat stopping place where one paradigm ends and another begins. At any given moment society holds a multiplicity of worldviews. In the current universe of our collective intelligence, several old paradigms and several new ones are all jockeying for dominance. Some are proving less useful and are diminishing among the population, while others are gaining in popularity as better possibilities. It is better, I think, that rather than speaking in terms of old and new, we simply acknowledge there is only current reality in which many different worldviews coexist.

themes are only too familiar with having our work derided as "too theoretical" or, worse yet, devalued as "another flavor of the month."

The worth of a new idea eventually proves itself by achieving better results or by offering a more sensible explanation of how the world works. As ideas become validated, criticisms gradually subside. Attacks are lessening all the time as companies achieve dramatic business results and strategic advantages from applying the new thinking.

However, the third social phenomenon is much more complex and harder to deal with—the temptation to simply incorporate the new perspectives into existing frameworks and tools. Even those of us who are convinced we are introducing something dramatically new and different can fall back into what is tried, true, and familiar. We may rearrange the deck chairs with new language, but we haven't at all made the conceptual leap from surface "ship" to "atomic submarine." Most of what we see in actual practice both as models and as tools, stems from old ways of thinking. People unconsciously try to simply stretch their old perspectives and tools to encompass the new ideas, and then wonder why they are not getting the results they hoped for.

What you find then is a very strange mix of old thinking and new language. For example, someone might suggest trying to understand knowledge processes with a flow chart. Or suggest trying to assign a dollar valuation to an intangible. These approaches simply don't work. Further, bad analogies and inappropriate tools may seriously mislead people or completely subvert the very principles that are being introduced. It takes courage, persistence, experimentation, and constant questioning of assumptions to continue to move forward from a new set of values and a profoundly different worldview.

TRANSLATING THE SHIFT INTO BUSINESS PRACTICES

Transpersonal psychologist Ken Wilber describes a radical change in our worldview as a "deep shift," which changes the very foundation of our understanding.[6] The "deep shift" that is happening at a societal level is the evolution of thought away from engineering toward living systems. The emerging worldview across a wide range of scientific disciplines is more dynamic and interconnected, drawing from newer sciences that speak of probabilities instead of prediction.

Whenever an individual or society undergoes this type of deep shift, our understanding expands. We see where our old assumptions and ways of operating were not necessarily wrong, they were just too small. A child learns to crawl, then to walk, and eventually to run. Some day she may learn to dance. The new ways of moving do not make the old knowledge of crawling or walking obsolete. Rather, foundational knowledge is integrated into an expanded worldview that offers an additional choice of "dancing."

Once our view expands, there is a period of "translation" in which we reorganize our theories and practices so that they will fit into the new worldview. We retire what has become obsolete, keep what will fit into the new perspective, and identify gaps in our understanding that we will need to address.

One way to visualize this process of deep shifts and translation is suggested in Figure 3.4. In the worldview at the bottom there may be an anomaly, something peculiar or different, that the current worldview cannot explain. Exploring such anomalies can serve as a gateway to the next order of understanding. Our questions literally pull us through the wormhole into a different, broader universe.

Once we are there, we have a higher order of understanding, in which the previous anomaly is now explained. This is like stepping to a higher rung of a ladder where we see more because the visible horizon has expanded. We then integrate this new worldview with the things we understood before, keeping some and discarding others that are no longer useful. Then, of course, once we are nicely settled in, we will probably notice yet another anomaly that the new view can't really explain. We explore again and once more experience a deep shift to a new explanatory theory and worldview in which that anomaly now makes sense. Again, we translate or rearrange what we knew before.

This movement to a new perspective often feels like a creative "Aha!" It is the moment when psychologist Carl Jung says we "know"

FIGURE 3.4   *Deep shifts and translation. Anomalies that we can't explain with current thinking act as gateways to the next level of thinking where they then make sense.*

—when new knowledge connects with old in such a way that both are transformed.

COLLIDING WORLDVIEWS

In light of the deep shift currently underway, Table 3.1 demonstrates a sampling of some of the colliding worldviews that we are attempting to reconcile in business and economics. The "pull" is toward the new thinking, yet we must somehow integrate or "translate" the old thinking and principles to determine their relevance and place in the new order.

Along with this evolution in economic thinking, a corresponding shift of thinking can be traced in recent management literature. We are seeing more socially and environmentally responsible values arising from a new sense of ourselves as global citizens. We now generally believe that we must treat people with respect and dignity to foster their highest creative efforts. New assumptions about knowledge as the primary economic resource are driving a managerial focus on knowledge and information.

TABLE 3.1   ColldingWorldviews[7]—Shifting Foundations of Economic Thinking

Assumption	Old Economic Thinking	New Economic Thinking
Economic Resources are …	Finite and limited to materials available from the earth's crust	Both finite and potentially infinite as ideas are created by human minds
Principle of wealth is …	No increase in actual total of material things	Total of knowledge and ideas increases
Underlying economic law is …	Diminishing returns due to scarcity of resources, resulting in increasing costs per unit	Increasing returns as replication of discoveries leads to falling costs per unit
Markets operate as …	Commodity markets based on same products and resources	Value-added markets based on distinctly different products and unique intellectual resources
Ownership means holding …	Property rights of things in perpetuity	Limited-time property rights of patents
Work is organized by …	Division of labor	Peer-to-peer networks
The operative system dynamic is …	The tragedy of the commons, when people share and deplete same resource	No diminishment of resource when ideas are shared
Primary economic goals are …	Efficient production, extracting efficiencies from labor and machines	Bolstering future discovery through development of human creativity and knowledge
Value creation occurs through …	Value chains of simple relationships, similar to a production line	Value networks of complex, interdependent, dynamic relationships
Economic indicators are …	Quantitative	Quantitative and Qualitative

This shift is causing a re-evaluation of virtually every aspect of organizational and economic life, from how we define value to questions of ownership, through the quest to find meaning and even "spirit" in the workplace. Consider though, that almost every analytical method and tool used in business and economics came out of the old industrial model and its underlying Newtonian worldview. This dynamic new world of knowledge and value will require a new generation of tools and lenses, as shown in Table 3.2.

The difference between these two worlds is readily apparent with these comparison charts (Tables 3.1 and 3.2). They are rooted in very different sciences and thus originate from quite different assumptions and perspectives. Both perspectives are useful for understanding events. Newtonian physics did not become totally obsolete just because we now understand some of the principles of quantum physics. It does, however, limit our understanding when we try to apply its principles to the behavior of complex systems such as organizations. Now that we understand more about complex systems, our challenge is to successfully and appropriately apply the insights and principles of *both* Newtonian physics and quantum physics.

TABLE 3.2 Shifting Worldview of Organizational and Managerial Thinking.[8]

Assumption	Old Management Thinking	New Management Thinking
Scientific foundations for management practice are ...	Newtonian physics, engineering	Quantum physics, natural and behavioral science
Management focuses on ...	Predictability and control	Understanding, insight, coherence
Worker relationships are ...	Employee based	Contract based
Information is ...	Ultimately knowable	Infinite and unbounded

TABLE 3.2 *(continued)*

Assumption	Old Management Thinking	New Management Thinking
Knowledge creation is ...	Individually focused	Collectively, collaboratively, organizationally focused
Ethical foundations are ...	Competition and individual survival	Cooperation and survival of the network
Laws of success are based on ...	Competition Dominance	Cooperation Relationships
Inner life is ...	Not relevant	Very important
Feelings are ...	Interference	Feedback, source of insights
Sense of time is ...	Monochronic (linear, one thing happening at a time)	Polychronic (nonlinear, many things happening at once)
We understand by ...	Dissecting into parts	Seeing wholes and dynamic relationships
Growth is ...	Linear, manageable	Organic, chaotic
Organizations happen ...	By design	Through emergence
Governance should be ...	Directed from the top	Distributed, democratic
Workers need to be ...	Specialized, segmented	Multifaceted, adaptive, always learning
Motivation is from ...	External forces or influence	Intrinsic creativity and core beliefs
Change is ...	Something to worry about	All there is

THE ORGANIZATIONAL DILEMMA

We are currently in a state of transition from one worldview to another. However, we face a dilemma. Because we have not completely adjusted our business models to the emerging worldview, we are experiencing emergent dynamics that we do not yet understand.

We cannot go back into the box of the mechanistic worldview; it doesn't work for us anymore for understanding the world of enterprise. Yet there are many things from that old perspective that should and will endure over time because they are valid and useful when applied to the right questions. For example, financial accounting methods are still very useful when applied to questions of revenue, costs, and profit. They are not so useful when applied to intangible assets. We need to integrate, not carelessly discard structures, processes, and systems that are working well. Our current need is for methods and approaches that will help us move into the new ways, while honoring and valuing our history. At the same time, we would like to find our way into these new perspectives without causing any more social upheaval than necessary.

So we are snagged on the horns of dilemma. The word *dilemma* comes from a Greek root meaning *two propositions*. Charles Hampton Turner describes a true dilemma as a situation for which there is no absolute answer; one must navigate between two forces, or "horns," of the dilemma in a continuous learning cycle. A classic organizational dilemma is the continual oscillation between whether it is better to centralize and consolidate functions, or to decentralize and create

---

Reorganizing Without Violence

Some change efforts are disasters, but not necessarily because they are attempts to do something new. The real pain and disruptions seem to happen when we carelessly dismantle the old systems that were working perfectly in a previous context. Historically, revolutionaries have been confronted violently by the old order. But we are seeing a new spirit of change in which dramatic reorganizations can occur without violence. An excellent example of this is the birth of the European Union. This may well be one of the rare times in history when there has been a major power shift involving multiple nation states without experiencing war.

redundancy. Hampton-Turner also points out that four to six dilemmas are the most that one group can deal with effectively.[9]

The shift of consciousness we are experiencing poses an underlying, or "meta-level," dilemma that influences the way we manage all the dilemmas we face. We cannot reason our way with the old logic, yet in many situations that old logic is still useful. On one horn of the dilemma is realization that organizations are complex systems that cannot be managed, engineered, or controlled. On the other horn of the dilemma sit all those business principles, processes, procedures, and systems we depend on that work in mechanistic linear ways. For those we must continue to operate with the old logic, at least to some degree. We may eventually be able to incorporate the new thinking even into many of those domains. But for the time being we must be very clear as to which worldview we are operating from and approach learning with a much higher level of self-reflection than has ever before been required.

It is pretty safe to assume that all of us function with both types of logic. We may identify more strongly mentally and emotionally with one view or the other, but we still hold both of them. Most people easily comprehend that something like the weather is complex and beyond human control. On the other hand, most of us find linear process thinking very useful when paying our bills and certainly want a well-engineered automobile when we drive our children to school.

Some people in business are already working from the new assumptions. But for the most part, we have not adjusted our business models, conceptual frameworks, and tools in the ways we need to in order to work with complexity. Since we have not, we find ourselves experiencing disturbing socioeconomic dynamics that we do not yet understand. If we acknowledge that this is our situation, then we will seek business tools that help us prosper in the face of this meta-level dilemma. We already have an excellent repertoire of engineering tools based on Newtonian logic. However, our indiscriminate use of them leads to partial solutions, needless bureaucracy, and suboptimization of the whole for the sake of the parts. We now need to master the skills and tools that will help us better understand true complexity.

OUR CREATIVE LEARNING QUESTIONS

Making this shift from a mechanistic viewpoint to a true systems viewpoint is a tall order for human society. It is happening not only in business and economics but along multiple dimensions. More important, each of these dimensions has both an inner-world shift of logic and assumptions and an outer-world manifestation that is expressed as new practices, behaviors, structures, and systems.

In order to meet this challenge, we have collectively posed creative questions for ourselves that will help develop the skills we need to be successful. We will take a brief look at some of the core questions, where we are now, and more significantly, which new frameworks, tools, methods, and practices are proving valuable.

CHAPTER ENDNOTES

[1] Paul H. Ray and Sherry Ruth Anderson, Ph.D., *The Cultural Creatives: How 50 Million People are Changing the World*, Harmony Books, 2000.

[2] Verna Allee, *The Knowledge Evolution: Expanding Organizational Intelligence*, Butterworth-Heinemann, 1997.

[3] Verna Allee, "Knowledge Networks and Communities of Practice," *OD Practitioner*, Fall–Winter 2000.

[4] Thomas S Kuhn, *The Structure of Scientific Revolutions*, 2nd Ed., University of Chicago Press, 1970.

[5] Max Boisot, *Information Space: A Framework for Learning in Organizations, Institutions and Culture*, Routledge, 1995.

[6] Ken Wilber, *The Atman Project*, (Wheaton, Ill: Theosophical Publishing, 1980).

[7] Verna Allee, "The Art and Practice of Being a Revolutionary," *Journal of Knowledge Management*, June 1999.

[8] Verna Allee, "The Art and Practice of Being a Revolutionary."

[9] Charles Hampton-Turner, *Charting the Corporate Mind: Graphic Solutions to Business Conflicts*, Free Press, 1990.

Our questions about knowledge, intangibles, and networks are creative questions that will guide us through complexity.

FOUR
Living Networks

The views expressed in this book, and the methods described in later chapters are informed by living systems theory. There have been many different metaphors used to describe organizations, from "well-oiled machines" to living organisms. The organic metaphor underlies early work by people such as Ludwig von Bertalanffy, who developed general systems theory. In business, people have been using a living systems analogy in regard to organizations since the 1960s. Many familiar management practices also draw on organic metaphors. The idea of the contingency plan, for example, is based on the assumption that organizations have a biological need to adapt to the environment.

Organizations have the characteristics of living systems. Like other living systems, organizations have awareness and cognition. They are open systems, interacting with and adapting to the environment. They process inputs and outputs. In the living, networked world of organizations, we must understand companies not as discrete entities but rather as elements in a socioeconomic ecosystem. Our understanding of other living systems can point us to the right things to look for in understanding business dynamics.

Characteristics of Living Systems

Let's first look at some of the key characteristics of living systems. Then we will explore how new management approaches are helping us understand and work with these elements.

Fritjof Capra, the noted physicist, defines three key criteria of a living system as *pattern, structure* and *process*.[1] The *pattern of organization* is the configuration of relationships among the system's components which determine its essential characteristics. Certain relationships must be present before something can be recognized as a leaf, a forest, a dog, or a tree. So one particular pattern of relationships tells us that we have encountered an organization, while another pattern would suggest a family.

The *structure of the system* is the physical embodiment of its pattern of organization. Seeing the pattern involves an abstract mapping of relationships, while a description of structure involves describing the actual physical components, their shapes, composition, and so forth. In other words, the pattern of organization might be a dog, but the structure determines whether it is a collie or a toy poodle. Organizations also exist in many varieties: health care associations, government bodies, dot-coms, churches, and associations, to name just a few. In organizations, structure also points to the purpose of a system, why it exists in the first place.

A third criterion is *process*. According to Capra, "The *process* of a living system is the activity involved in the continual embodiment of the system's pattern of organization. Thus the *process* criterion is the link between the *pattern* and *structure*."[2]

However, those three conditions alone (pattern, structure and process) could also describe a mechanical system. What makes something a truly living system? There are two additional criteria that must be met:

1. The pattern of organization in a living system is consistent with that of an autopoietic network. An autopoietic network is one that continually produces itself, so that the being and doing are inseparable. That continual process of producing is cognitive in nature. In theory, all living systems are cognitive, and cognition always implies the existence of an autopoietic network. In busi-

ness this is referred to as organizational intelligence. We will take a closer look at organizational intelligence later in this chapter.

2. Living systems are also dissipative structures that are open to the flow of energy and matter. Dissipative structures exist on the edge of chaos. With too much openness they disintegrate; with too little they become rigid and closed and can no longer exchange energy and matter with the environment. In business, these types of energy and matter exchanges are of an economic order: exchanges of goods, services, revenue, and intangible economic exchanges such as knowledge and favors that have value to others.

This view of living systems draws from the work of Chilean biologists, Humberto Maturana and Francisco Varela. Through research into cells and the functions of the nervous system, they make a convincing argument that the basic act of knowing, or cognition, does not simply mirror an objective reality "out there". Instead knowing is an active process, rooted in our biological structure, by which we actually create our world of experience.[3]

BUSINESS AS A LIVING SYSTEM

The basic pattern of all living systems, including organizations, is the network. Networks are sets of nonlinear, nonhierarchical relationships that nest with other networks.[4] In any living system, the *pattern of organization* is essentially the *network*, regardless of whether we try to temporarily force it into some other type of pattern. The pattern of organization is closed or it wouldn't be an organization, but the *structure* is open. So, in business we find individual organizations may vary in structure and form, but their essential pattern is still that of an organization.

The process of life defined by Capra as the continual embodiment of an autopoietic pattern of organization is identified with *cognition, the process of knowing.* According to this theory, mind is not a thing, but a process of interacting with the environment through cognitive actions.

Human social systems, of course, have very advanced cognitive processes, including symbolic language and conceptual abstractions. When we ask questions about how knowledge is created, sustained, shared, and applied, about how decisions are made or how a business learns, we are trying to understand the cognitive processes that support the continual renewal of an organization.

The criteria indicate that working with an organization as a living system would require having ways to:

1. Identify its pattern of organization *as* an organization.
2. Describe its structure.
3. Discover its most critical processes from *both* a cognitive perspective and the flow of energy and matter.

This appears to be a tall order, and feels suspiciously like it might be a lot of work. It would be quite difficult if one tried to pin down or describe absolutely everything that is going on. Fortunately, humans are very good at working with incomplete information, so we don't have to go to those lengths. People can work with a partial model and still reach major breakthroughs. Later, I will demonstrate a way to describe any organizational structure, and its critical processes, using a mapping technique.

For now, we can use these characteristics of living systems as a framework to show how different management issues are actually efforts to find new ways of describing the organization as a living system. We are stepping from our old business ideas and practices into the new things we need to focus on to understand complexity. The questions we pose are gateways into future knowledge.

is no longer at the helm? Upon closer examination, one finds that a particular identity and character are constantly renewed through storytelling and through regular support for desired behaviors. So leaders with certain characteristics continue to emerge from the larger collective consciousness of that particular organization.

Governance

One form of this inquiry into identity and its relationship to structure is focused on governance, the way guiding principles and agreements are developed and supported in an organization. Experiments range from incremental changes such as attempting to distribute or share leadership, to the creation of an organization such as the Society for Organizational Learning, where governance is decreed by a collaboratively developed "constitution."

One of the drivers for the new focus on governance is the issue of transparency. The digital economy has created an environment where private decisions and action can instantly become public. Everyone in a company must be accountable for ethical business practices, as errors in judgment are quickly held up for public display and scrutiny. The potential for disaster exists when questionable practices suddenly become front page headlines. The provocative *Cluetrain Manifesto*, which first grew on the Internet and then was published as a best-selling book, flatly declares that the world of business is a public conversation where everybody talks with anyone and everyone.[6] There are no secrets, and ethical behavior and reputations are essential for survival. Character really does count.

Questions about structure essentially are questions about relationships. A structure is defined by the characteristics of its nodes or components, their relationships with each other, and the interactions between them. Structure then isn't the conceptual business model, the organization chart, the legal structure, or the buildings and office furniture. Organizational structure is the set of essential and defining characteristics of the enterprise that describe its unique physical embodiment as an organization.

We also need to remember that organizations are a social phenomenon. What that means is *we just make them up*. There is no one "right" organizational form or structure. Organizations are expressions of human social systems, self-organizing to obtain the resources needed to survive and realize their full potential. Understanding structure requires exploring both the visible world of behaviors, relationships, and forms, and the invisible world of values, identity, and beliefs.

ORGANIZATIONAL INTELLIGENCE

Living systems always have two important process aspects of life: (1) cognitive and (2) material. The material process aspect has to do with the way energy and matter are exchanged across boundaries and processed through the system, and is discussed in the next section.

Organizational intelligence is the cognitive ability of the organization to be aware of itself and its environment and to devise beneficial ways to interact with that environment. James March, the noted scholar who has done extensive research on organizational intelligence, says *"An intelligent organization is one that adopts procedures, that consistently do well (in the organization's own terms) in the face of constraints imposed by such things as scarce resources and competition."*[7]

Cognitive Pathways

One facet of cognition is how new information is taken in and exchanged across boundaries. How is a company able to sense and respond to its environment? When people in one part of the organization become aware of something that is happening in the environment, how does that awareness get transferred across the company?

We are looking closely at the way knowledge "travels" across enterprise boundaries, internally and externally. How can we better support organizational "neural networks," especially at the critical synapses where knowledge and ideas transfer from one person or group to another?

Learning

The other facet of cognition is the way the organization learns or processes information to its benefit. How are knowledge inputs transformed into new learning and knowledge? All organizations learn. How well they learn and benefit from information is directly related to the ways people interact with each other and with their environment. Some organizations are more advanced than others, and there are facilitating factors that can improve an organization's learning capacity.[8]

Understanding organizational intelligence requires understanding how collective intelligence and learning operates in groups of people, and in social systems. We are now trying to understand how we can better support knowledge creation and sharing in a way that improves the quality of learning across the organization.

Extensive research into organizational intelligence and learning has made it clear that decision making and knowledge creation are not rational processes, but social processes. People have explored group decision making as a way to address collective intelligence since the 1960s. Such processes are much messier than we have acknowledged and the implications of that are enormous. Across networks, natural decision making is really not centralized at all, but is *distributed*. Efforts to centralize decision making and the creation of bureaucracy actually work against organizational intelligence!

More recently, our questions have further expanded to looking at the results, or outputs, of decisions and learning—the accumulated organizational knowledge that persists over time.

A related question is how knowledge becomes so embedded in the physical and social systems of the company that it remains accessible to the company even if a key individual leaves. All of these are questions about organizational intelligence. They are helping us rethink both the human aspects of organizations and the technology infrastructure that enables knowledge creation and dissemination.

As the knowledge economy continues to evolve, material aspects become less important and the cognitive aspects become critical for success. Now it is important for managers to work as deliberately to improve the quality of knowledge and learning as it is to improve the quality of products and services. Indeed, in this economy they are often one and the same.

ECONOMIC EXCHANGES

In addition to cognitive processes, living systems have processes for exchanging energy and matter. In business terms, these processes would be what we ordinarily think of as economic exchanges. At one time, we would have thought of economic exchanges only in terms of physical goods and resources, and money or capital. However, we are now starting to understand certain intangibles also, as economic exchanges, meaning they have value.

We can see now that a company can gain economic benefit from its cognitive ability to transform information and knowledge inputs into learning and value. Organizations evolve by economizing on their consumption of natural resources, and knowledge is the primary natural resource used to do that. Examples are the way knowledge-intensive technologies such as miniaturization and nanotechnology reduce demand of physical resources.[9]

A corollary question is how can a company leverage its cognitive capabilities to create benefit for others? Nonphysical economic exchanges such as services, knowledge, and experience make this economy quite different than it was a decade ago, and we are struggling to understand the new guiding principles. The intense interest in intangible assets is forcing people to rethink their business and economic models. Even financial accounting bodies and the governmental bodies in Europe are grappling with the questions of how to measure, value, and appreciate (in the sense of grow) intangible assets, including knowledge.

Marketplaces are changing and so are the exchanges that take place within them. Complementary currencies such as flier miles and service hours are challenging our old ideas about money. As systems mature they become more diverse, and the global economy is no exception. New business models emerge when people rethink the way they handle business transactions, sometimes rewriting the rules of business in their industry.

Our questions about economic exchanges have also expanded, from a narrow focus on private enterprise to questions about the economic disparity between rich and poor nations. People are seeking ways to speed development of disadvantaged populations into the knowledge economy and increase access to technologies and social goods.

We are also beginning to examine environmental exchanges in economic terms. Companies such as Royal Dutch Shell are beginning to actively report how they are contributing to, or detracting from, the health of the environment, and are reporting the success and failures of corporate ethics. Sustainable business practices are becoming corporate assets, as people increasingly vote with their purchases for companies that embody high personal and social values. As a wider range of activities are viewed as economic exchanges, we will continue to find new pathways for redefining and developing corporate success, true wealth, and prosperity. More on this in Chapters 10 and 11.

When we trace the pattern of our current questions about organizations, we find they are all questions dealing with some aspect of a living system. We are posing creative questions for ourselves that will help us learn our way into understanding and supporting the health and vitality of the socioeconomic order as a living system.

CHAPTER ENDNOTES

[1] Fritjof Capra, *The Web of Life: A New Scientific Understanding of Living Systems*, Anchor Books, 1996.

[2] Fritjof Capra, *The Web of Life: A New Scientific Understanding of Living Systems*.

[3] Humberto R Maturana, and Francisco J Varela, *The Tree of Knowledge: The Biological Roots of Human Understanding*, Shambala, 1987.

[4] Fritjof Capra, *The Web of Life: A New Scientific Understanding of Living System*.

[5] See the Glossary. Term adopted by the Chaordic Alliance based on the work of Dee Hock, founder of VISA. www.chaordic.org.

[6] Rick Levine, Christopher Locke, Doc Searles, and David Weinberger, *The Cluetrain Manifesto: The end of business as usual*, Perseus Books, 2000. www.cluetrain.com.

[7] James G. March, *The Pursuit of Organizational Intelligence* (Introduction), Blackwell Business Press, 1999.

[8] Anthony J DiBella and Edwin C Nevis, *How Organizations Learn: An Integrated Strategy for Building Learning Capability* (San Francisco: Jossey-Bass, 1998).

[9] Max Boisot, *Knowledge Assets: Securing Competitive Advantage in the Knowledge Economy*, Oxford University Press, 1998.

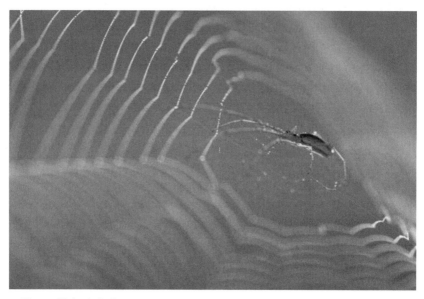

© *2002 Hemera Technologies Inc.*

In the living, networked world of organizations, we must understand companies not as discrete entities but rather as elements in a socioeconomic ecosystem.

FIVE
Learning into Complexity

What does it really mean to work with the new network patterns of organization? What will be the shape of the knowledge we will need? We have only to look at the questions we ask. It is what we *don't* know and are trying to understand that opens the portal to the next level. We are not only trying to master the more complex modes of knowledge, we are also deepening and broadening our understanding and skills in every domain of knowledge. We are learning to pay attention differently and developing a whole new range of tools and practices to help us.

Meeting the Challenge of Complexity

Living systems—and organizations—are complex adaptive systems. What exactly do we mean when we say something is complex? David Snowden of the Institute for Knowledge Management (IKM) makes a simple distinction between the merely complicated and the truly complex. "An airplane is complicated," he says. "When something is complicated it has many different parts and interactions. However, those parts and interactions can be known, understood, engineered, and managed. When something is truly complex there are simply too many variables for it to ever be truly known, fully understood, or managed." Life is complex. Organizations are complex.

However, we have tended to treat companies and organizations as if they are merely complicated, not complex. One cannot engineer a

61

complex system, yet for years we have talked about our companies and organizations as if we can somehow step outside of them and tinker with them, model them, manage them, or engineer them. We try to manage complexity by focusing on only one small area at a time, breaking things down into separate functions and processes. That might be useful for understanding something complicated, but it simply doesn't work with things that are complex, such as organizations.

When something is truly complex, all the parts work together in such a way that the whole cannot be divided without losing its integrity—and the parts also lose their integrity when separated from the

---

Complexity Theory

Complexity concepts and theories are increasingly being used, both metaphorically and literally, in a business context. What is complexity theory? Well, the answer to that is rather complex. No, really—it is. It is an umbrella term that refers to the interdisciplinary exploration of a set of theories from different fields, all of which share a focus on complex adaptive systems and evolution. Not all complex adaptive systems are living systems. Some of the contributing sciences are physics, biology, chemistry, sociology, cybernetics, nonlinear dynamics, nonlinear mathematics, and chaos theory. When we are specifically discussing organizations, that mix would also include psychology, anthropology, and organizational behavior.

This lattice of disciplines has contributed many terms and concepts that could readily lend themselves to our business language and are slowly creeping into business vocabulary. Business analysts are beginning to refer to complexity concepts such as co-evolution, self-organization, edge of chaos, strange attractors, dissipative equilibrium, entrainment, mutation, recombination, and feedback.

whole. When you cut a cow in half you don't get two cows. You get a mess. Noted organizational expert Russell Ackoff refers to any truly complex situation as a systems "mess." Everything seems to be connected to and dependent on something else.

WORKING WITH COMPLEXITY

Organizations are an interesting intersection of complicated mechanistic systems that are "engineered" according to Newtonian physics, and human systems that are organic, self-organizing, and complex. We must draw from several different disciplines to be effective in organizational life. For example, application of linear thinking, control functions, and task specialization (e.g., dissecting workflow) does lead to great efficiencies in processes for manufacturing, logistics, and order fulfillment.

Whole-systems thinking, on the other hand, helps us understand dynamic relationships and how everything is working together so we can make good business decisions. It brings an ability to work with multiple interdependent variables, including the complex universe of human hearts, minds, and intelligence. When thinking systemically, our old process engineering tools and statistical controls are not going to be very useful.

Learning to work with complexity will require more than changing what we do; it will also require a shift of mind. Our culture has powerful values and preferences for individual achievement, scientific specialization, and linear thinking. These values are seemingly at odds with what will be required for living in a complex world. Yet, somehow we must learn to live with new mindsets and methods if we want to find our way to a future that works for everyone and will sustain us all.

No one person can fully understand a complex system. That requires multiple lenses and multiple minds. We seek meaningful patterns to help us understand and take effective action. We must look upward and outward to the external behaviors and features that we can observe in the organizations we are part of. At the same time, we must look downward and inward to understand the underlying assumptions, beliefs, and values that drive our actions. We must be able to work deliberately with underlying assumptions and to see how they play out in our behaviors, while respecting the dynamic relationship between our thought world and creations.

We cannot change or manage a complex adaptive system directly. As individuals we can only manage our roles, our activities, our relationships, and how we participate. While we cannot manage a living network, it is important that we understand its dynamics. By doing so, we can manage ourselves in ways that serve us and support the vitality and health of the whole.

Heuristic Tools for Sensing Patterns

The world of predictability, or what we thought was predictability, is now behind us and we must live in a world of probabilities. We have left behind the deterministic economy of physical goods and the production line and are now in a knowledge-based economy that behaves very differently. We can see patterns, but they are always shifting and we can never predict what will happen next. Such an environment requires heuristic approaches that feel very new and different for most people.

Heuristic inquiry is reflective, nonjudgmental, and experimental in nature. It encourages exploration of what we don't understand. Heuristic inquiry does not mean fuzzy thinking. Done well, it is every bit as rigorous a management discipline as the more familiar engineering approaches. And the discipline of heuristic inquiry offers the capacity to be comfortable and effective in a world of multiple possibilities and uncertainties.

We need to employ all our senses to find the patterns in complexity, asking ourselves not only how we can view a complex situation but also how can we feel it, taste it, touch it, and experience it. We need to bring our talents for metaphor, poetry, and music to bear. Emotional responses are feedback, providing important information about healthy behaviors and effective practices.

Simplexities: Patterns and Principles for Understanding Complexity

Along with heuristic inquiry, it can be very helpful to explore observable external behaviors using more visual and structured modeling, mapping, and diagnostic techniques. However, the only way in which these can really be useful is to employ them as tools to support inquiry, rather than to seek rules and laws, control, or predictability. Visual mapping approaches, coupled with thoughtful reflection, can be especially powerful in helping a group reach shared understanding of what is happening.

When we look for patterns and principles in a complex system, we are seeking what I think of as *simplexities*. Simplexities are simple patterns of relationships and principles that can be used to understand or model enormous complexity. They describe foundational elements of a complex situation or system.

For example, the pattern of DNA is an example of a *simplexity*. The basic structure of DNA is four chemical elements arranged in a double helix formation. These strands of DNA are woven into complex networks of genetic information that encode the life patterns for every living thing, from bacteria to primates, including humans. Every cell in your body has a complex network of DNA. Considering the number of cells in your body (about 30 to 50 trillion with about 6 inches of DNA in each one) it would take an airplane several centuries to fly the length of all that DNA if it were stretched out end to end.[1]

While discovering a simplexity is helpful, there are limitations. The detection of the protein coding of DNA mistakenly led some people down an engineering path, assuming that we now understand the building blocks of life. When the basic code of the structure was unraveled after two decades, we did find ways to manipulate that code in a quest to cure genetic disorders. However, life simply doesn't operate according to mechanistic principles. Early efforts in "engineering" or cloning have demonstrated that the clone does *not* develop exactly like the original, even though the genetic code is the same. We may understand a little about the genetic alphabet, but we don't understand the syntax, the grammar, or the language of life that it is part of. Life is complex and greater than its parts. The part of DNA that we do understand, the protein coding, is really only 3 to 5 percent of the entire DNA molecule and its interactions.[2]

If we respect their limitations, simplexities can help us work more effectively in the complex world of business. A business example is the pattern of *the process*. Seeing process patterns has proven to be very helpful in gaining efficiencies and improving the quality of goods and services. The same simple principles apply to virtually any kind of process, from claims processing to product launch. But managing processes does not ensure a healthy company. There are many other variables that affect success such as market conditions, the economy, competition, workforce competence, and brand image. Nonetheless, being able to see and work with processes gives people a way to attend to and communicate certain principles and interactions that we may want to work with.

This is how people typically work with complexity—by developing methods and tools to illuminate key patterns and principles. Flowcharts help us describe processes. We model formal reporting relationships with an organization chart. We might use social network analysis to reveal informal relationships and knowledge networks. The protocols and standards of the Internet allow infinite linkages to be created in infinite combinations. Simple rules and road patterns allow millions of automobile drivers to self-organize several million complex traffic routes a day, mostly without bumping into each other. All these practices and standards are also simplexities, simple principles, sets of relationships, and rules that can support enormous complexity.

Today we are seeking simplexities, tools, and methods that help us see whole-system patterns and dynamic relationships. We are trying to learn the simple and essential principles of healthy and adaptable organizations. Our larger sense of universal interdependency is creating a sense of urgency to find ways of working that nurture vitality across multiple systems—our own organizations and the larger economic, social, and physical ecosystems that we are part of. We can't pay attention to everything, but if we can learn to hold a systems perspective, we will find tools and methods to help us pay attention to what matters. We need to find the simplexities that will help us work successfully in a complex world.

WHERE WE ARE NOW

So, where are we now? What have we learned and what have we mastered? Today our questions cover every mode of knowledge, as we prepare ourselves for true global citizenship. All knowledge is important and interconnected. We must have capacity in all the different forms, or modes, of knowledge complexity in order to be successful human beings or successful organizations.

Table 5.1 provides a quick overview of where we are in our learning journey. The continuum of knowledge, complexity, and learning that

TABLE 5.1 *Checklist of What We Are Learning at Each Level of Knowledge Complexity (Allee).*

What We Are Learning	Knowledge Mode
We are devising global mechanisms and simple protocols for transferring data and information, and for simplifying transactions.	Data
We are creating pathways and networks, such as the Internet, that follow the principles of living systems, to link and hyperlink information. We are creating rule-based, "intelligent" software for managing content, finding and disseminating information, and finding patterns in the data.	Information (procedures)
We are enabling functions and tasks with just-in-time learning, e-learning, knowledge portals, and best practice repositories. People are using these tools to weave the web of knowledge that supports the organization.	Knowledge (functions)
We are beginning to notice and support learning communities and knowledge networks from which new knowledge emerges and from which we create meaning and context for applying what we know.	Meaning (context)

TABLE 5.1 (continued)

What We Are Learning	Knowledge Mode
We are slowly but surely developing the capacity for whole-systems thinking and for better understanding the relationships between our mental models and the organizations we create.	Philosophy (systems)
We are finding that an organization's character, identity, purpose, and values really do stand for something and are at the heart of a successful enterprise. They serve as the "strange attractors" that draw people together. They are catalysts for growing the unique structure and form of the enterprise.	Wisdom (renewal)
We are finding new urgency in creating a world that works for all and that preserves the global commons of the environment. We are shifting our identity and values individually and collectively to become global citizens.	Union (sustainability)

this table is based on is not a hierarchy; it is simply a framework. (See the Appendix for more information.) Hierarchies are an order we impose on the world, but the web of human knowledge does not know hierarchy.

We have already discovered a number of new approaches and principles that are proving useful as business moves to a more knowledge-intensive focus. These emerging principles, values, themes, and concepts bring real business results. The new tools and approaches are different, but they are not unduly difficult. As with any set of new skills, there is a learning curve, but we are finding more ways all the time to keep things on track without overly complicating them.

THREE LEVELS OF PRACTICE

The seven-mode continuum of complexity presented in the Appendix can be simplified into three basic levels of practice: the operational, the tactical, and the strategic. Every level of practice is based on new ethical underpinnings for success. We will discuss those issues as we go, and we will elaborate on some of the most critical leadership principles and ethical issues in Chapter 14.

Each of these three levels of practice addresses a different key question (see Figure 5.1). Emerging business practices include several applications that are proving to be exceptionally useful. It is interesting to note that some type of network perspective or technology supports each level. At the strategic level it is the value network. At the tactical level it is social networks. At the operational level, technology networks form the backbone of the digital technologies that support day-to-day tasks. Further, each of these involves a different type of learning and requires different tools to support that level of work.

Operational Level

Network principles underpin the new technologies, such as the Internet, that help us adapt and innovate faster. Digital technologies enable conducting key business transactions and activities in an electronic environment, driving down transaction costs. Content management is migrating from traditional databases to dynamic portal environments.

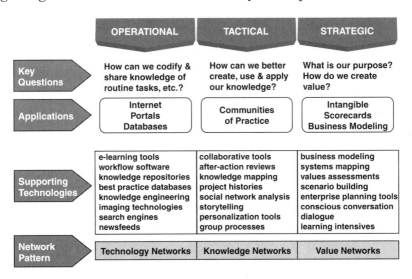

FIGURE 5.1 *Three levels of questions for organizations to address, with tools and technologies that are proving useful.*

These more flexible technologies adapt to the ever-shifting web of knowledge and allow continual renewal and updating.

At the operational level, new technologies also support the codification and delivery of learning and just-in-time knowledge to individual workers. We are acquiring new competencies for capturing knowledge and documenting work as we go; packaging content for different learning styles, cultures, and media; and providing just-in-time e-learning modules that complement traditional classroom learning.

Tactical Level

At the tactical level, the new thinking revolves around knowledge networks and communities of practice. We are realizing that no matter what its purpose, a firm's success depends on its ability to create and apply knowledge more effectively than its competitors. However, knowledge is a very different kind of resource than oil or timber, and the old rules of production no longer apply. The unit of production for organizational knowledge is both individual and communal. While teams are still important, communities of practice and knowledge networks are the "killer applications" for intelligently creating, sharing, and applying knowledge.

The tactical level is about creating the context for the work that is done. We are learning about the social aspects of transferring learning and best practices, creating knowledge, and developing competencies. These depend on group activities that support the making of meaning, including storytelling, mentoring, and coaching. It is important to begin evolving normal group collaboration and team learning processes toward true communal learning, where knowledge and insights arise from, and are shared with, the whole group and with the entire enterprise.

Strategic Level

One of the major shifts at the strategic level involves rethinking value to include both monetary value and intangible value. The new thinking about intangibles, intellectual capital, and nonfinancial forms of value surfaced only during the past ten years or so. Yet already, understanding intangibles has become one of the most important business and economic questions, not only in the United States and Europe but all over the world.

Along with this new perspective is a complementary focus on enterprises as webs of business relationships. The traditional view regards each enterprise as a lone competitor, scrambling for a niche in its business ecosystem. Now we are beginning to regard every enterprise as a node in complex interdependent value networks, where success comes through collaboration, cooperation, and creating a business environment where everybody can be successful, including competitors. We are learning new network principles to guide our actions.

Strategic level practices also include group reflection and dialogue to address questions that arise regarding corporate ethics, purpose, and identity, or big-picture issues and situations. We have gradually seen an increasing emphasis on "conscious conversations" as tools to reach better decisions regarding strategic direction.

Leadership teams preparing for the new economy will find themselves engaged in challenging, provocative, and sometimes baffling and paradoxical situations. The following chapters address a number of insights and new practices that are emerging at each of these three levels. Those companies willing to learn and explore these questions will build the adaptive capacity needed for success.

CHAPTER ENDNOTES

[1] Elisabet Sahtouris, "Living Systems, the Internet and the Human Future," Presentation, Planetwork, Global Ecology and Information Technology, San Francisco, May 2000.

[2] Elisabet Sahtouris, "Living Systems, the Internet and the Human Future."

Learning to work with complexity will require more than changing what we do; it will also require a shift of mind.

PART II

*Operational
Enterprise
Knowledge*

SIX
Power and Limits of Technology

The Internet is the backbone of the Knowledge Economy. To appreciate both the power and the limits of this core technology, we need to understand how the Internet is accelerating the shift in the economic foundation from the physical to the nonphysical, and recognize how the world conversation is changing (and not changing).

The physical, or "hard," economy is based on traditional goods and products that are the outputs of machines and production lines. The "soft" (nonphysical) economy is based on intangibles such as experiences, ideas, and relationships. Commentator Kevin Kelly, editor of *Wired Magazine* and author of *New Rules for the New Economy*, predicts that all businesses, even those whose primary output is something physical like steel or automobiles, will soon be built around soft resources and technology.[1]

Every single industry has been affected, first by computer technology, and now by the capacity of the Internet to move and distribute information in the blink of an eye to any computer on the planet with a modem. Everything we do is going digital. We are rapidly approaching the time when computer chips will even be embedded in our clothes.

Andy Grove of Intel predicts that by 2005 every company will be an Internet company. Staying ahead requires understanding how networks prosper and how soft goods and resources serve as the new foundation for value creation.

The Conversation Is Changing

The Internet is not simply about information—more important, it is about communication. Information is meaningless unless there is a receiver that can interpret and use the information to take effective action. Without communication there can be no life. Even at a cellular level, organisms are in constant communication with each other. Internet technologies have expanded communication capability among humans to a degree we could not have even imagined, and are allowing the true networked pattern of human communication and of organizations to emerge.

The Internet is also allowing a different type of communication to take place in human society. It is a world conversation, not limited by time or space. It is also an open conversation that is not under the control of any one state, government, or corporation. The Internet is subject to prevailing laws governing commerce and crime but has yet to be regulated to any significant degree. It hosts a conversation so extensive that it is becoming nearly impossible for governments and corporations to keep secrets, especially dirty little secrets (e.g., cooking the books or dumping toxic waste).

This conversation is open to anyone who can get on line. The Internet is home for mainstream media such as CNN and *Fortune*, but it is also a mechanism for amplifying the smallest of voices that may have previously have been shut out. We can hear the voices of the poor, logging in from a lone computer owned by an entire village; voices of underdeveloped countries and political minorities; voices of local fishermen who are outraged at an unreported oil spill. Everyone is talking to everybody. This is enabling new forms of social organization and new patterns of sharing knowledge and information.

In other ways, conversation hasn't changed. There is always the issue of credibility and trust. People still need face-to-face contact if they would engage more deeply with each other. People thought that all this connectivity would lead to less air travel because more business can now be conducted at a distance. Instead, travel went up. People are making new contacts and friends at a distance, yet still need face time to build the deeper relationships and trust that support working together.

THE GREAT CONVERSATION OF BUSINESS

This intense global conversation is changing business in dramatic ways. People are talking with each other in e-mail exchanges, instant messages, chat rooms, forums, and through personal Web sites and shared workrooms. They talk about everything: their dogs, their children, politics, war, poverty, the environment, music, movies, celebrities, events, scandals, fads, trends, complaints—and (gasp) the products they buy. Log on to a conversation of Saturn automobile owners, and you may find participants enthusing over their gas mileage or comparing costs for service at their local dealerships. Everything goes public—the good, the bad, and the really ugly.

Just the existence of a public conversation among Saturn owners suggests that people can learn more from each other about issues with their automobiles than they do from the company. Companies speak in bland, homogenized, corporate speak that has been polished by the marketing and the legal departments. Human conversations have an unmistakably different voice, one that is messy and honest, sometimes grumpy, and often very funny. These are the voices that people turn to when they want to know what is really going on.

People holding Internet conversations also work, for the most part. They work in pharmaceutical companies, in software companies, department stores, oil refineries, libraries, and schools. They work for real companies, they work for *your* company, and they work for your competitors. They'll jump to the defense if they think their firm got a bad rap. If they aren't happy or were just laid off, they just might spill the beans about the real reason people can't get their parts on time.

For business, the implications of these public conversations are enormous. The bestseller *Cluetrain Manifesto* was a real wake-up call for a lot of companies.[2] The book actually appeared first on the Internet as a discussion between the authors about how the Internet is affecting business. They make a powerful case that companies that are tuning into these conversations and learning to participate are getting smarter faster. People are looking for substance and honesty and for real people to talk with about their business needs.

This is all pretty scary for most companies. After all, they've controlled business communication for a long time. People learned what was going on inside a company by reading the annual report, press releases, or marketing ads, finding out only what the company wanted them to know. Now companies have lost control over the messages. The truth will find a way out and all the glossy advertising in the world cannot reshape it or pull it back.

Companies must now learn how to be transparent. They must learn how to be in real conversations with their customers, suppliers, partners, stakeholders, stockholders, and the public. Real communication doesn't come from broadcasting messages; it comes through real two-way conversations.

The Internet and Network Principles

Many people have pointed out that the success of the Internet has much to do with the way it self-organizes according to network principles. Networks are quite simple at one level. They consist of just two elements: nodes and connectors. The value and capability of a network expands with the number of connections. In the case of the Internet, connections increase as nodes or members increase. In other types of networks, such as a developing brain, the number of connections increases faster than the number of nodes.

When a certain level of connectivity is reached in a complex system, the capabilities that are being unleashed may be far greater than the sum of the parts. Such capabilities can be thought of as "emergent"—they emerge spontaneously when certain conditions are met. For example, certain types of cognitive processing become possible only when the brain reaches a sufficient number of neural connections.

Now a technological neural network is growing and self-organizing into greater and greater capability as it blankets the whole earth. What new abilities might we develop as the neural pathways of the global brain become richer and denser?

One new capability that comes to mind is an ability to gain instant feedback and awareness of global conditions. A couple of years ago there was a spate of destructive forest fires in Indonesia. At first, the fires were blamed on weather conditions. Then a group of students tracked down satellite photos and land maps on the Internet. They found an interesting pattern in that the lines of the fires followed property lines of certain landowners who had been trying to get permits for land clearing. Once this pattern became public, social pressure brought about an end to the burning.

About that same time, I participated in a videotaped panel discussion for the Institute for the Future. We were exploring the positive ways the Internet could contribute to the health and well-being of the planet. In the course of the discussion, I posed a scenario by asking, "What if the Audubon Society uses their Web site to gather daily or weekly bird counts instead of waiting for their annual Christmas Day count? We would be able to see variations in songbird populations, indicating environmental stress, before the situation rose to dangerous levels. Then, also through the Web site, members could organize to collectively apply pressure, locally and globally, to address the problem. This would mean having much earlier awareness and response than ever before." When I reached home after the session, out of curiosity I popped onto the Audubon Society's Web site. Much to my embarrassment, the "scenario" I had posed was not a scenario at all. The Society had already implemented that very type of bird counting capability on its Web site!

Information fuels intelligence and sparks innovation. The more connections that are made, the greater the sources of information and innovation; the greater the influence and reach of the network, the more intelligent it becomes.

The Internet and Organizational Structure

Connectivity can lead to dramatically different patterns of organization. In biological history, one of the biggest turning points in natural history occurred when neurons evolved. Neurons are biological connectors that help cells communicate. Before there were neurons, cells had to be very close to each other, in little blobs, to coordinate their functions. Neurons enabled cells to communicate from a distance, which allowed an infinite variety of life forms to emerge. Thanks to neurons, cells can be rearranged and assigned different functions. Cells can collect into all sorts of different shapes, from fish to flowers, hummingbirds to humpbacked whales. Now, with the Internet, we might anticipate a similar expansion in the variety of economic and organizational forms. Kevin Kelly poses the possibilities for us:

> *Silicon chips linked into high-bandwidth channels are the neurons of our culture. Until this moment, our economy has been in the multicellular stage. Our industrial age has required each customer or company to almost physically touch one another. Our firms and organizations resemble blobs. Now, by the enabling invention of silicon and glass neurons, a million new forms are possible. Boom! An infinite variety of new shapes and sizes of social organizations are suddenly possible. Unimaginable forms of commerce can now coalesce in the new economy. We are about to witness an explosion of entities built on relationships and technology that will rival the early days of life on Earth in their variety.*[3]

An amazing number of possibilities of form may now be possible, but certain features of organizations still persist. Business people assumed that the information age would automatically lead to leaner, flatter organizations. This has not happened, much to the surprise of some early enthusiasts. Workplace sociologist Paul Attewell exposes that assumption as a myth by demonstrating that the number of nonproduction employees in manufacturing has steadily *increased* as the workplace as become more digitized. And the percent of managerial workforce has also increased![4]

But what has happened is not a surprise at all, if one realizes that information is not knowledge. The information age has actually increased the demand for human intelligence to generate, interpret, and apply all the information in meaningful ways.

Less Collection, More Connection

One of the primary requirements for supporting knowledge work is to ensure that people have the tools and information they need to complete their everyday tasks. But another, equally important goal is to provide appropriate technologies for collaborative work in a complex global environment. The more complex modes of knowledge work cannot be turned over to databases and automation. They are accomplished by people through active and immediate conversation

---

Information or Knowledge?

The discussion about the distinction between knowledge and information has been going on intensely for several years now. Some of my own work on this question, which is briefly summarized in the Appendix, was the foundation for my book, *The Knowledge Evolution*. My premise in that book is that information, knowledge, and wisdom are not discrete but are way-stations along a continuum of complexity. The pattern surfaces so predictably that I refer to it as The Knowledge Archetype. It is quite clear to me, after several years of dialogues, that there will never be a universally agreed definition for either knowledge or information. However, the question of how knowledge is different from information will always surface the same core *pattern of understanding*, even though it never seems to show up twice in exactly the same way or in quite the same words.

Given that, let me state that in my view there is no such thing as *pure* information, data, or knowledge. The only raw data we ever receive is at the physical, sensory level. Beyond that, anything we recognize, notice, experience, convey, or communicate is subject to our *social* experience as humans. Anything that is shaped as human communication is an expression of our social experience and consciousness. Even the way we interpret raw sensory data is dependent on the culture we grew up in, the language we first learned to speak, and the perceptions and interpretations of those around us. The process of interacting with the environment and interpreting our experience moment by moment is a seamless social, cognitive, and physiological process of knowing.

Information, in popular usage, generally refers to anything in verbal, written, or symbolic form that can be read, viewed, heard, and comprehended by another human being. For purposes of discussions in this book, that definition will work fine. However, from physical sensations to abstract philosophies, all interpretation and understanding is social in nature.

and interchanges. Connective technologies enable us to link up with our peers so that we may weave the threads of our understanding together into new synthesis and insights.

The networked world of business keeps getting more global. Twenty years ago, most people worked in the same location and time zone as their co-workers. Information resources were usually in the same place, in filing cabinets or in the on-site IT department. Office technologies were facsimile machines and desktop computers, mostly for word processing and accounting. Gradually, computers and software became more sophisticated, and, with e-mail capabilities, the workplace opened up.

Now, as the network pattern of organization becomes more dominant, working on projects with people in other locations has become routine, and more work is becoming distributed and virtual. A recent survey indicates that more than 40 percent of projects in Fortune 1000 companies are performed in an environmentally distributed setting.[5] This virtual work brings challenges of time, space, and culture, as people work across time zones, across geographic boundaries, and across different cultures (see Figure 6.1).

Connectivity is the key. Companies that understand the conversation of business and network behaviors are putting more emphasis on collaborative technologies. Knowledge management expert Larry Prusak likes to say, "If you have a dollar to spend on technology, spend it connecting, not collecting."[6] People now expect to have available distributed-project management capability, real-time Web-based meeting spaces, high-speed connectivity, laptop computers, cell

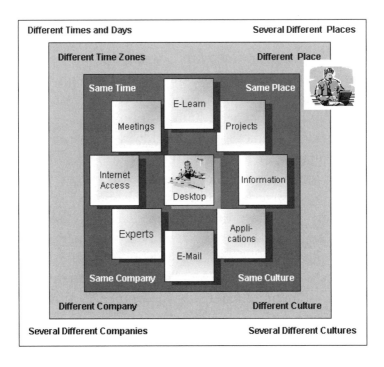

FIGURE 6.1   *Technology needs change as work becomes more distributed across time, space, culture, and organizations.*

phones, conference calling, and a whole range of communication technologies.

E-Business Expands the Conversation

Electronic business (e-business) is also becoming increasingly connective. Many people think e-business is about selling things over the Internet. But only one particular type of e-business focuses on using the Internet for transactions, marketing, and branding—e-commerce.

Another area of e-business is supporting core business processes, such as supply chain management. An example of this is Federal Express's handling of logistics, allowing customers to track packages and closely manage their own accounts.

A third area of e-business is partnering with other companies and researchers to create or expand product and service offerings. This demands high connectivity for technology and for people. Cisco was an early adopter in going on line with as many business processes and relationships as possible. Cisco uses the Internet for supply chain management and customer interfaces, and also uses it extensively to handle employee recruiting and benefits administration.

CIO Magazine predicts that worldwide business-to-business e-commerce will increase from $282 billion in year 2000 to $4.3 trillion by 2005.[7] That is an astonishing annual growth rate of 73 percent. In such a deeply interconnected world of organizations, the most important technologies are those that support shared workspaces, project management, and databases that can work across multiple platforms. In most cases, these must be accessed by people who have varying levels and types of technology and different languages. Different cultures will be connected, sometimes company-to-company, without crossing national boundaries.

FREEING INTELLIGENCE FOR GREATER CHALLENGES

Digital technologies have fueled a knowledge explosion by moving tasks that used to be complex to the routine, thus freeing up our intelligence to move on to more complex questions. For example, banking transactions used to require untold man-hours to post, calculate, and communicate daily transactions. Now, although banking has been extensively automated, bank employees have not disappeared. On the contrary, digital technologies have expanded the types of services that can be offered, opening up more advanced knowledge work to create, design, market, sell, and customize services.

Information technologies have a very high degree of utility for routine tasks. But as knowledge becomes more complex, the usefulness of technologies drops (see Figure 6.2). Routine tasks, such as filling out and processing forms, can be easily codified and documented. Call centers use software that can present a customer's entire purchase and service history, display responses for routine questions (and some unusual variations), and make suggestions for selling additional products to the customer. However, human thought and creativity is required for more complex tasks. Unusual situations require an original human solution, and initiating new services is a very human process drawing on digital technologies primarily as a source of data.

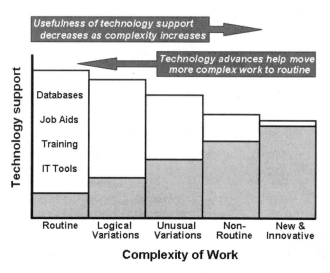

FIGURE 6.2 *Usefulness of technology declines for more complex work. (Adapted from Karl Wiig.)*[6]

The really big technology win has been enhancement of individual productivity. As we saw in Chapter 1, we have seen a very real improvement in productivity with the advent of digital technologies. However, many companies fail to realize as much advantage as they might, because they don't really turn that freed-up intelligence resource loose on other, more complex problems.

TECHNOLOGIES DISTRIBUTE CONTROL

The story of technology in organizations follows the trend of control moving away from the center. First, the IT department acted as a corporate gatekeeper for knowledge and information, since highly specialized skill was required to manage a database. IT designed and maintained the database—the way data was structured, the boundaries of the content, and the way content was displayed. The needs of an individual user or a small group of users were usually passed over. More IT attention would go to larger, "more important," projects serving larger numbers of people or serving those groups that have more political power.

Now knowledge creation, access, and control have become more decentralized and democratic. This movement from centralized to decentralized control began to change in the 1990s with the development of simpler database software products, desktop spreadsheet programs, and document management systems. Now people could design and manage their own data systems without having to petition the IT group. Consequently, the IT function was able to devote more of its time to integrating hardware and software systems across the enterprise.

The shift toward more distributed management of knowledge continues through the ongoing development of Web technologies. Internal corporate e-mail systems appeared early on and are still the most widely used intranet technologies. It is estimated that 8 billion e-mail messages will flood U.S. corporations each day in 2002.[9]

Today, it is hard to conceive of any large global corporation that does not have an intranet. Intranets are private versions of the Internet that are protected from the external Internet environment by firewalls. They began popping up extensively in 1995, which is still quite recent in business history. Extranets quickly followed. These are intranets that extend to the larger business community, including customers, suppliers, and business partners.

Both intranets and extranets have become more sophisticated, often with full Web capabilities, including search engines and Java-based Web applications. The development of the Java computer language in the mid-1990s sparked a flurry of small applications (applets) that can be accessed through any computer operating system.

Using these technologies, individuals and groups can easily create, populate, and manage their own Web sites. Workgroups, project teams, and special interest groups can control the production of their own knowledge resources. Business units use intranets and the Internet to access corporate databases, repositories, libraries, shared filing spaces, applications, and published content in different media. Now the means of production for knowledge work is available to anyone with a computer and Internet connection.

Companies now have a wealth of tools to choose from to meet the information demands of the business. Many technology vendors have positioned their products as knowledge management technologies. They are a good foundation for any company and many of the new technologies are essential for knowledge workers. However, information and content management does not automatically lead to wiser decisions, innovation, or even knowledge sharing.

Technology Is Not Enough

The right technologies alone are not enough. Other types of infrastructure are just as important as building the right technology backbone. Let me give an example.

Portals

Most of us use some type of portal, such as Yahoo, to access the Internet. Portals are software applications that manage end-user, customized access to multiple information resources and applications. More capabilities are being developed for portal technology all the time, including means to track usage and preferences. Some of the typical features are represented in a screen capture from Plumtree, a well-known vendor for portals, in Figure 6.3. Portal technologies are becoming simpler all the time. The design and maintenance of a portal is increasingly controlled by the group of users that use the IT department as a resource, rather than turning over all responsibility.

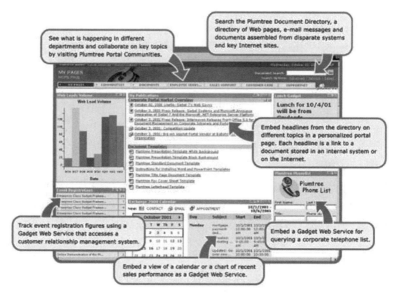

FIGURE 6.3   *Example of an enterprise portal from Plumtree. Gadgets are small Web-based applications that can be accessed through the portal. Portal features include links to documents, other Web sites, discussion groups, and newsfeeds as well as to other enterprise systems and software. (Courtesy Plumtree Software.)* [10]

One large global company that I work with was trying to encourage greater knowledge sharing and innovation across the company. The company was getting hammered by its competition, a much younger company from another country and culture. As we began exploring the client's knowledge-sharing practices, we found barriers everywhere. The company did not even have an integrated e-mail system. Where it did have intranet technology, there were firewalls—not just between the company and the outside but even between business units and departments.

Going a bit deeper, we found that there was an explicit company policy concerning knowledge sharing. People seeking knowledge had to be able to demonstrate why they needed a particular piece of information. Needless to say, this slowed down things greatly. The policy was quickly reversed—any employee could ask for anything and get it. Instead, anyone who wants to hoard information has to prove why that it necessary. It was a beginning, but the firewalls and policies were indicators of a problematic culture steeped in mistrust and internal competition. The best technology infrastructure in the world cannot overcome other cultural and structural barriers.

The technology arena is one of the easiest places to squander a lot of money on tools that are only marginally useful. By the same token, it is one place where the right investments can reap big benefits. But at its heart, improving organizational intelligence is not a technology question—it is a human question.

Technology enablers are absolutely essential for any enterprise that wants to thrive in the networked world of organizations. There must be a technology infrastructure in place that really will support the right kind of conversations and connections. Companies also need an integrated technology foundation that will allow people to document their work and processes, build learning modules, develop specialized portals, create shared files and content, manage their e-mail, and locate both internal and external resources.

Once the right technology foundation is in place, how do we get people to actually make use of tools that are available? We know that building something doesn't mean that people will use it. What other infrastructure needs and behavior habits must be addressed to support networked organizations, facilitate connections, and keep the conversations flowing? We will consider these issues in Chapter 7.

CHAPTER ENDNOTES

[1] Kevin Kelly, *New Rules for the New Economy: Ten Radical Strategies for a Connected World*, Viking Press, 1998.

[2] Rick Levine, Christopher Locke, Doc Searles, and David Weinberger, *The Cluetrain Manifesto: The end of business as usual*, Perseus Books, 2000. Also see www.cluetrain.com.

[3] Kevin Kelly, *New Rules for the New Economy: Ten Radical Strategies for a Connected World*.

[4] John Seely Brown, and Paul Duguid, *The Social Life of Information*, Harvard Business School Press, 2000.

[5] David Coleman, "Distributed Project Management Comes of Age," http://www.collaborate.com, 2000.

[6] Larry Prusack and Tom Davenport, *Working Knowledge*, Harvard Business School Press, 1998.

[7] "B2B Commerce to Eclipse $4 trillion by 2005", *CIO.com*, November 2001, www.cio.com.

[8] Wiig, Karl. "What Future Knowledge Management Users May Expect." *Journal of Knowledge Management*, vol. 3, no. 2, 1999, p. 157.

[9] David Longworth, "Finding E-Content Contentment," *Destination CRM.com*, December 4, 2001.

[10] Plumtree Software, www.plumtree.com. © 2002 Plumtree Software, Inc. All rights reserved.

Internet and digital technologies are allowing the true networked pattern of human communication and of organizations to emerge.

SEVEN
The Web of Knowledge

Digital, Web-enabled technologies are helping to weave together the natural human webs of knowledge that support people in their work. At the operational level, any enterprise needs to ensure that each worker or workgroup is able to access, create, manipulate, and utilize the information resources and tools that are particular to their tasks.

However, one thing we do know for sure is that just installing good technologies does not mean that people will use them. More than one company has found itself with millions of dollars invested in best practice databases that never get off the ground, or that just limp along with a few stalwart contributors and users. Others in the organization either don't know the resource exists, don't know how to use it, or just don't have the time or interest to participate.

The shortcomings and failures of technology systems have sharpened our curiosity about how knowledge really does work in organizations. Clearly, there is an enormous reservoir of know-how, skills, and knowledge that underpins any successful organization. How then do we tap into that resource and leverage it across a global organization?

THE UNITS OF PRODUCTION

Most disappointing results are not from a failure of technology but from a failure to understand that the real units of knowledge production are both the individual and the collective. This is one of the primary places people go awry in trying to support knowledge workers. They get it wrong on both parts of an equation. One side is push: creating and disseminating knowledge. The other, the demand or pull side, is understanding where, why, and how people seek knowledge resources. In between lies the social process of sense making.

Individuals carry most of the burden of knowledge production. They are the ones who must actually execute the tasks of the business—process documents, complete the paperwork, develop drawings and documents, package internal and external knowledge products, and communicate and distribute the work. However, no individual works in a vacuum.

The other unit of knowledge creation is the community of peers that socializes about the work that they do, identifies knowledge gaps, and works together to identify or create the resources to fill the gaps. So while individuals produce and package most knowledge resources, the market and context for that work resides in the community of peers and other stakeholders that care about the quality of that work and are affected by it.

This dual aspect of the unit of knowledge production is typical of the way knowledge dynamics are rich in paradox. Knowledge in organizations is a world of koans, myths, and riddles. Melissie Rumizen, author of *The Complete Idiot's Guide to Knowledge Management,* and I like to collect and dissect knowledge myths and paradoxes. Some of these can cause quite a bit of confusion and wasted effort. With any myth, of course, there are some ways it might be true as well as not true. There are three myths that are especially troublesome when it comes to knowledge sharing.

MYTH 1: PEOPLE DON'T WANT TO SHARE

There seems to be a general assumption that people don't want to share knowledge. In one sense this is true. People are so busy and overloaded with responsibilities that simply taking the time to participate in some type of knowledge-sharing exercise can be a challenge. When manag-

---

The Koan

A koan is a teaching paradox that is used to train Zen Buddhist monks. The form of a koan is usually a statement, with a corollary that is an opposing statement. For example:

Koan: Whatever you say a thing is—it is.
Corollary: Whatever you say a thing is—it isn't.

Meditating on these statements reveals ways that both are true. Whatever we say a thing is—does indeed state our *experience* of what it is. So in that sense the first statement is true. The corollary is also true, that whatever we say a thing is—at some level it isn't that at all. Personal experience is just one of many possible ways something might be experienced or known. So with that meaning the corollary is also true. We are in the realm of paradox when two apparently opposing statements can both be true.

---

ers blithely suggest that people need to do more knowledge sharing or populate a knowledge repository, they often don't consider or allow for the real amount time it takes to do that.

If people do find the time to support knowledge sharing, they have widely different abilities to communicate. If using a knowledge technology such as a best practice database requires writing something, even with templates and an editor only a few people have writing skills adequate for the task. Then too, those with good communication skills may not be the most expert or knowledgeable on the subject.

If knowledge sharing takes the form of mentoring and coaching, that also is a skill set that people may or may not have. Cross-functional training is one method of transferring knowledge, but many companies find their culture, time constraints, and reward systems simply don't support that approach without some major overhaul.

So, on one hand it might appear that people don't want to share what they know. On the other hand, people love to talk about their work. Just about everyone likes to tell stories about a recent project or show another person how to do something. There may be a few cases where people would feel their job might be threatened if they taught it to someone else, but that resistance often is about something else going on in the organization that is getting in the way.

One early leader in knowledge management, Arian Ward, insists that people love to share what they know. The real problem is all the organizational barriers that stand in their way. He suggests looking for what keeps people from sharing, rather than just pushing them to share more. For example, the whole culture and infrastructure could be oriented toward individual achievement, so that helping another negatively affects achieving one's own performance goals. Functional boundaries and reporting structures may be so rigid that people rarely work with others outside their immediate work group. There are dozens of ways that people may be unconsciously rewarded for not sharing.

It is best to assume that people find an intrinsic benefit in sharing knowledge and that they generally do enjoy learning from one another. Then, focus attention on the corporate infrastructure, policies, systems, rewards, culture, and corporate values that may be influencing behaviors.

MYTH 2: WE NEED TO MAKE TACIT KNOWLEDGE EXPLICIT AND SYSTEMATIZED

Another assumption one frequently comes across is that the goal of supporting organizational knowledge is to make tacit knowledge explicit so that it can be systematized and made available to others. Early practitioners talked a lot about tacit and explicit knowledge, so people picked up these terms and began using them in a variety of ways.

The concept of tacit knowledge traces back to the philosopher Michael Polanyi, who seriously explored the tacit dimensions of knowledge. However, the way most people use the term is not how Polanyi thought of tacit knowledge at all. In common usage, people refer to tacit knowledge as what is in people's heads, and to explicit knowledge as tacit knowledge that has been codified and communicated. In general thinking, the tacit or unspoken knowledge that people have is a rich storehouse or memory bank that should be opened up so the knowledge can be extracted, codified, and shared with others.

However, Polanyi's tacit dimension refers to innate intelligence, perception, and capacities for reasoning—rather than a type of memory or knowledge store. So for Polanyi, tacit knowledge could never be made explicit, nor does it need to be. His position is that tacit knowledge sharing underlies *any* act of communication, in the form of unspoken commonalities around very basic perceptions and human interaction. In his view there is no linear progression of knowledge from tacit to explicit; they are two aspects of the one process of knowing. Thus, when knowledge is shared there is an articulated or explicit communication and an unspoken tacit communication going on at the same time.[1]

So how did people get this idea that tacit knowledge needs to be made explicit? It arose from thinking of tacit knowledge as stored memory, experience, or content that simply hasn't been articulated. This is actually much easier for people to grasp than Polanyi's dimension. And even though it is not Polanyi's view, it is a very useful idea for helping people think about knowledge sharing.

This usage showed up in the popular book, the *Knowledge Creating Company*, in which authors Nonaka and Takeuchi describe the process by which tacit knowledge is made explicit. In their view, the process of knowing is a social process whereby tacit knowledge—that which is embedded in people's experience—is socialized or shared through direct experience. That shared experience can be articulated into explicit concepts that can then be systematized into a knowledge system. Once systematized, that now-explicit knowledge can be learned by others and once again become embedded in experience as tacit knowledge (see Figure 7.1)

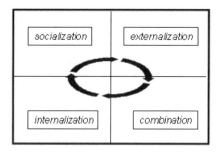

FIGURE 7.1   *Nonaka and Takeuchi's spiral of knowledge creation.*[2]

Socialization is the direct conveyance of tacit knowledge through shared experience.

Externalization is the process of articulating tacit knowledge into explicit concepts.

Combination is the process of systematizing concepts into a knowledge system.

Internalization is embodying the explicit knowledge into tacit operational knowledge.

This is not the tacit knowledge described by Polanyi as basic innate capacities. Rather, Nonaka and Takeuchi are using the term to designate unarticulated personal knowledge or skill that could be made explicit by deliberate effort. Since Nonaka's work in particular is widely read and admired, this usage has become quite common in knowledge management circles.

It might be a bit more accurate to describe the myth as "all *personal* knowledge needs to be made explicit." That, it would seem, better fits with the assumption of many people that the real knowledge problem is getting all that personal knowledge that is in people's heads into codified forms that can be captured, stored, and disseminated.

So does this tacit, unspoken personal knowledge need to be made explicit? Yes, many times. Those who are particularly masterful at a skill are good candidates to help develop job aids and guidelines for other people who are attempting the same task. People who have led a

Explicit Knowledge

While we are grappling with terms, what do people mean by *explicit* knowledge? Explicit basically means fully defined, explained, or formulated. The word actually has its roots in the Latin word meaning *to unfold*. In the popular sense, people think of explicit knowledge as knowledge that is communicated and shared with others. That does not mean communication only through documents or media, although some technology vendors seem to imply that. Knowledge can be communicated through movement, facial expression, and any symbolic language such as words, mathematics, drawings, and stories.

different type of project than usual can be very helpful to others if they share their experiences through storytelling, written project histories, informal conversations, or coaching sessions with others who undertake similar projects.

Of course, not all personal experience is of equal value to a company. We don't need to know what route salespeople take to an appointment, but it might be useful to know the selling context they walk into and how they handle it. Those are things that others can learn from.

The art is to know what things can be made explicit and are worth the effort. The corollary is to realize that tacit knowledge can be communicated and shared in a variety of ways, and does not necessarily need to be articulated or codified.

Myth 3: Documentation Is the Key to Sharing Best Practices

The most popular approach to knowledge sharing is to focus on sharing best practices. Such efforts tend to get very good results. A recent study shows that fully 45 percent of high-impact knowledge management projects have sharing best practices as a primary goal.[3]

Sharing best practices became a popular learning approach with the rise of benchmarking in the early 1990s, as a key component of implementing total quality. However, a strange phenomenon surfaced rather quickly. Companies would initiate and complete a study, then get the same request from a different division of the partner company a few months later. Sometimes people would begin a study, only to learn that another operating unit in their very own company was considered best in class. A 1994 study by Gabriel Szulanski, Assistant Professor of Management at Wharton, found that practices could reside in a company for years before transferring to other parts of the organization. Even when recognized as a best practice, it still takes *over two years* on the average before other sites take it up, if at all.[4]

If successful, however, there is no question that sharing best practices can bring excellent business results. The use by Texas Instruments of best practice sharing realized a savings of $1.5 billion in chip fabrication yield, enough to dump plans for a whole new plant. Ford Motors' best practice sharing effort has added $1.2 billion in value since 1996. Ford now has over 2,800 practices accumulated on Ford Web, its shared practice database, with over 5,500 replications a year.

Myth 3 Subset: Technology Replaces the Need for Face-To-Face Sharing

As useful as databases might be, person-to-person knowledge sharing is the key. Nancy Dixon, author of *Common Knowledge*, has studied best practice sharing and finds that many technology-based sharing systems quickly evolve to a combination of technology and face-to-face meetings. For example, Ford's Best Practice Replication process sends groups of people on reciprocal site visits and then debriefs those visits to identify and document best practices.[5]

Oil companies such as British Petroleum, Shell, and Chevron have all realized enormous cost savings through best practice sharing, and all emphasize person-to-person knowledge sharing as the best way to do that. Chevron alone has saved over $1 billion since 1993. The experience of Chevron is fairly typical. Their practices have evolved from simple benchmarking studies in the early 1990s to a rich and varied menu of knowledge sharing methods in more than a dozen key focus areas. Jeff Stemke, leader of Chevron's knowledge initiative, describes several practices including:[6]

- *People networks.* Cross-company communities and networks are created to collect and share best practices in a specific area.
- *Cross-enterprise teams.* Teams within Chevron are deployed to another location or business unit to learn new methods.
- *Cross-pollinating.* High-level managers circulate around the world, visit sites, and learn best practices.
- *Share fairs.* Periodic, larger meetings are dedicated to showcasing outstanding practices that are broadly applicable across the enterprise.
- *Database technology.* Chevron's best practices sharing database is used widely across the enterprise.

Myth 3 Subset: Best Practices Don't Need to Be Copied Exactly

Gabriel Szulanski and Sidney Winter[7] have recently challenged another myth. They looked at an interesting phenomenon that happens as a result of sharing best practices—the surprisingly high failure rate of companies that try to reproduce a best practice. They found that in their enthusiasm to adopt a practice, people try to go one better and do something different or try to piece together parts of a number of different practices. Their hope, of course, is to create the perfect hybrid or set a new standard of excellence.

Many businesses need to replicate processes and practices at multiple locations, so this type of knowledge transfer is quite common. However, the research shows that people are woefully undisciplined when it comes to adopting another way of doing something when the goal is to leverage existing knowledge rather than create new knowledge. People are also undisciplined on the documentation side, often leaving out complex relationships or subtle points because they are just too difficult to explain. As a result, people trying to implement a practice from documentation are quite likely to get it wrong.

Not only does documentation need to be carefully constructed, the process or practice itself needs to be copied exactly, before changes are made. There are any number of ways people tinker with a process or begin customizing it too early, even in the process of setting it up. People tend to overestimate how much they know and inadvertently compromise the integrity of the process, impede quality or efficiency, and, in the worst cases, even create safety hazards.

Szulanski and Winter insist that a shared practice must be replicated as exactly as possible before starting to make any changes. A replica provides important benchmarks and measures that determine whether the knowledge transfer has been successful. There is a built-in coherence in the process that creates systems and subsystems that work together smoothly. The wisdom embedded in complex processes may not be apparent right away. Also, when something goes wrong it is important to be able to retrace your steps. It only makes sense to get good results with a proven process before beginning to make changes.

Intel takes this approach with its "Copy Exactly!" method to transfer semiconductor know-how from the first factory to subsequent ones. This is a complex process, and it is sometimes difficult to resist making changes. However, experience has shown that changes lead to more difficult problems down the road. Once again, we are learning that anything truly complex cannot be broken down into its parts without losing the integrity of the whole.

How People Really Share Practices

During the past few years, people began to take seriously the question of how people make sense of what they do and how they learn from each other in the workplace. One respected researcher, Etienne Wenger, has studied a number of workgroups and communities of shared practice.[8] Among those he looked at were claims processors. Many of the problems faced by processors have to do with figuring out such things as what a form signifies, how to represent a complex situation on a form that forces simple responses, why similar claims elicit different disbursements, assessing qualifications, and so on. The company, of course, offers documentation and explanations, but from the processor's point of view a rote answer is not helpful for meeting similar situations in the future.

Xerox's technical field representatives faced a similar challenge. John Seely Brown and Paul Duguid detail the story in their book, *The Social Life of Information*.[9] In the mid-1990s, researcher Julian Orr conducted an ethnographic study of the field reps who service the company's copiers at customer sites.[10] He found that the system of error codes (intended to help the reps identify the problem and find the right response in the machine documentation) was completely inadequate from the reps' point of view.

Technically, since copiers are machines, they are supposed to work predictably. The reality, especially in larger machines with numerous subsystems, is that every machine and model has its own peculiarities that reflect its age, condition, and patterns of use. Sometimes the prescribed "fix" didn't solve the problem. Other times the documentation did reveal the right solution, telling the reps what to do, but not why.

So what would the reps do to find answers to their problems? Simple—they would talk with each other. Orr found that the real beginning of a rep's day was not the first service call but breakfast beforehand—with fellow technicians. This highly social group would also get together for lunch, and sometimes on their own time at the end of the day. Interspersed with social activities and gossip, they talked about work continuously. This was the way they kept each other up to date, shared what they were running into, and what they were learning. It also built social ties so that when they ran into real trouble they would call each other for suggestions and help.[11]

CHALLENGING THE MYTHS

Based on their studies, Orr, Wenger, and other researchers are making a convincing argument that polishing and documenting processes is simply not enough. Equally important is the aspect of *practice*: the conversations about sense making and meaning that are required to carry out a process in everyday work.

Further, they found that many of the important linkages in the social web around the practice were not officially sanctioned but cut across organizational boundaries. Since this wasn't the way things were supposed to happen, the Xerox reps did a little improvising to make it look as though their solutions were arrived at according to plan. So not only did the real learning process not fit the official picture, it was hidden so that the fiction of the process could be maintained.

These findings of Orr and Wenger began knocking over myths about organizational knowledge like bowling pins. The Xerox reps were sharing a great deal of personal tacit knowledge, but they were doing it through storytelling, not by documenting and systematizing everything they were doing or learning. And it was clear that this group of technicians loved sharing knowledge—so much that they were taking personal time to do it. So the myth that people don't want to share knowledge was clearly unfounded in this instance. They were easily sharing tacit knowledge, and the existing approach to documentation of processes was clearly inadequate.

They also knocked over the two subset myths about sharing best practices. Clearly, the technology approach in place to solve errors did not reduce the need for fact-to-face interaction, so that myth also went by the wayside. Further, in practice people exactly replicated what someone else suggested before they moved on to adapt it or try something else. The exact replication of the practice was essential to the learning process, both individually and for the group.

It took a few years for people to really get it. After all, these are particularly troublesome findings in a business environment that assumes that the right technologies will solve all the knowledge challenges in the organization. However, with the explosion of interest in knowledge management in the late 1990s, the door was open to learn these lessons on a large scale.

When knowledge management hit the business community, companies found they were creating best practice databases and implementing portals and search engines without getting the results they had hoped for. However, every single one of the top companies in knowledge management, including those reporting the most outstanding business results, takes a communities of practice or network approach. Something very powerful is at work here, and people are eager to learn more about it. We will take a closer look at this in Chapter 8, but first let's see what Xerox did for its technicians.

EUREKA—XEROX GOT IT!

As a result of Orr's study, Xerox stopped trying to support the reps with more information from outside its community and began reinforcing internal ties. The first step was to provide reps with two-way radios so they could continue to talk with each other even when apart. The second step was to try to extend the reach of local solutions by setting up the Eureka best practice database.

Databases for technical information are nothing new. What is different about Eureka is that it is populated by the community of reps rather than by technical experts from outside the community. Of course, the database would become useless fairly quickly if people could just stick in any old idea or their favorite method. So Xerox established a peer review system from within its own community. A rep submits a tip, peers review it, and if it proves useful it is added to the database. Usefulness is determined by feedback from the rep community on whether they use the tip and how helpful it is.[12]

Figure 7.2 shows a screen capture of the Eureka system as it would be viewed from the laptop of a service rep. The arrows point to features such as the names of the author and the validator, access to search capabilities and other databases, and the success rate for the solution.

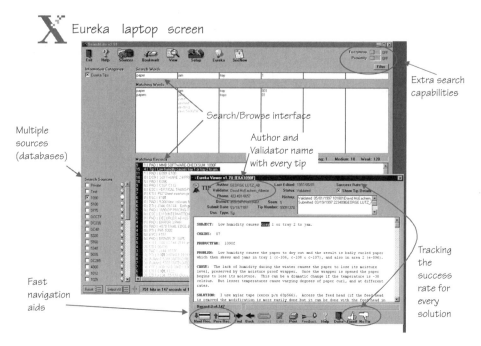

Eureka laptop screen

Extra search capabilities

Multiple sources (databases)

Search/Browse interface

Author and Validator name with every tip

Tracking the success rate for every solution

Fast navigation aids

FIGURE 7.2   *View of the Eureka best practice sharing database for technical service representatives servicing copiers at customer locations. (Courtesy Dan Holtshouse.)*[10]

However, what is important here is not the database but the very human processes that support it. What Xerox has done is put the practice above the process, as can be seen in Figure 7.3, which is one of Xerox's diagrams used to describe the Eureka community and database. Rather than rigidly enforcing a technical process, Xerox has allowed both the process and the practice to evolve together. The aim is to reinforce the internal ties among representatives, rather than discourage them. Sometimes the best solutions emerge from noticing what is really happening and working with it in a way that brings even better success.

In Chapter 6, we took a look at the way technologies such as the Internet are helping organizations more easily evolve to their natural network pattern as living systems. The research described in this chap-

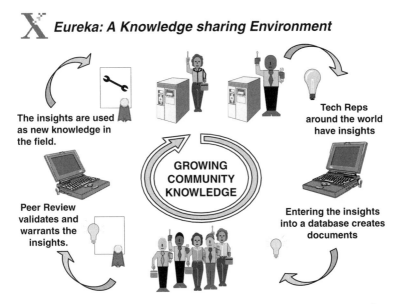

FIGURE 7.3 *Growing community knowledge by supporting a community of practice.*[11]

ter is demonstrating that the knowledge resource, which is fundamental to this economy, is itself deeply embedded in and inseparable from the networks and social communities from which it emerges. There is no question that fine-tuning business processes brings practical results. However, the really big breakthroughs on the knowledge side will not come from formal processes but through supporting people in the natural ways they weave the living web of knowledge.

CHAPTER ENDNOTES

[1] Michael Polanyi, *Personal Knowledge: Towards a Post-Critical Philosophy*, Chicago University Press, 1958, 1962.

[2] Ikujiro Nonaka and Hirotaka Takeuchi, *The Knowledge Creating Company: How Japanese Companies Create the Dynamics of Innovation*, Oxford University Press, 1995.

[3] Carol Hildebrand, "Making KM Pay Off," *CIO Enterprise Magazine*, Feb 15, 1999.

[4] Gabriel Szulanski, *Inter-Firm Transfer of Best Practices Project*, American Productivity and Quality Center, Houston, Texas, 1994.

[5] Nancy M. Dixon, *Common Knowledge: How Companies Thrive by Sharing What They Know*, Harvard Business School Press, 2000.

[6] Jeff Stemke, "Using Best Practice Teams and Communities of Practice To Accelerate Innovation Deployment," *Braintrust 2000*, Scottsdale AZ., February 2000.

[7] Gabriel Szulanski and Sidney Winter, "Getting it Right the Second Time," *Harvard Business Review*, January 2002.

[8] Etienne Wenger, *Communities of Practice: Learning, Meaning and Identity*, (Cambridge University Press, 1998).

[9] John Seely Brown and Paul Duguid, *The Social Life of Information*, Harvard Business School Press, 2000.

[10] Julian Orr, *Talking About Machines: An Ethnography of a Modern Job*, IRL Press, 1996.

[11] John Seely Brown, and Paul Duguid, *The Social Life of Information*.

[12] John Seely Brown, and Paul Duguid, *The Social Life of Information*.

[13] Dan Holtshouse, "The Knowledge Advantage," presentation for *OD Network Annual Conference*, October 2000.

[14] Dan Holtshouse, "The Knowledge Advantage."

© 2002 Hemera Technologies Inc.

The units of knowledge production are both the individual and the collective.

PART III

*Tactical
Approaches for
Sense Making*

EIGHT

Knowledge Networks and Learning Communities

Knowledge cannot be separated from the human networks and communities that create it, use it, and transform it. In all types of knowledge work, even where technology is very helpful, people require conversation, experimentation, and experiences shared with other people who do what they do. Especially as people move beyond routine processes into more complex challenges, they rely heavily on their colleagues and friends as thinking partners.

Our personal knowledge evolves as the conversations we are part of shift and change. Every conversation is an experiment in knowledge creation—testing ideas, trying out words and concepts, continuously creating and re-creating our experience of life itself.

For professionals and knowledge workers, conversations with their peers are particularly important. It is through such conversations that people fine-tune their knowledge and expertise. Since every field changes so quickly with new discoveries, we need each other to make sense of what we are doing, to create the context for our work, and to find better ways to go about it.

In a special study for the IBM Institute of Knowledge Management, researcher Rob Cross identifies five ways that networking[1] facilitates creation and use of knowledge:

1. People get answers to their questions, both know-what and know-how.

2. They receive meta-knowledge: pointers to domains of knowledge, databases, and people.

3. They find ways to reformulate their problems.

4. They receive affirmation and validations of their plans or solutions.

5. They gain symbolism (prestige) from contact with a respected person.

COMMUNITIES AND LEARNING

Since social interactions are so important for knowledge sharing, there is now a growing interest in practice communities, learning organization principles, networks, communities of practice, and social network analysis. We are expanding our focus from teams to patterns of teaming and community formation. We are getting better at understanding how people come together, work on projects, participate in communities, connect with networks, then disband and move into other webs of relationships.

Valdis Krebs, an expert in social network analysis, originated the diagrams shown in Figures 8.1, 8.2, and 8.3[2]. He has been applying social network analysis specifically to challenges of knowledge sharing. He finds that what is most critical to the success of a knowledge network is not the number of connections, but the *pattern* of the connections. Some patterns are helpful for knowledge sharing and some are not.

We learn from each other through building networks and communities. The network is the most natural and powerful vehicle for creating and sharing knowledge. But not all learning networks are alike.

Knowledge Networks and Communities of Interest

Most of us are part of at least one, and usually several, informal knowledge sharing networks. We know people we can call who can point us to good information or to other people who might have the answers to our questions. In an informal network people talk one-on-one but rarely gather and share in larger groups. Such networks don't really have clear boundaries or a beginning point but go on over time. Although they have the characteristics of social networks, they are a bit different because the knowledge, gossip, sharing, and stories are all about a particular topic.

Knowledge networks and business networks are sets of informal relationships in which connections are always shifting and changing. The primary purpose of informal networks is to collect and pass along information. There is no joint enterprise that holds them together, such as development of shared tools. They are just a set of relationships.

Communities of interest are also informal networks, only with a little more focus. They evolve organically and may be more deliberate about keeping each other informed. We might have a loose network of friends, neighbors, and family who share our interest in some hobby or passion, such as gardening or golf. There may even be a sense of community as people meet each other to socialize about events they may be attending, or to share a newsgroup. There is a common domain of interest, but people aren't deliberately engaged in learning as a community or improving their expertise together.

Knowledge networks and communities of interest, of course, can also be found in the workplace. They might extend outside the boundaries of the firm to include others who have overlapping interests with those inside the company. Today, many people working for a company's success aren't even "in" the company. They are customers, suppliers, business partners, contract workers, or consultants. Yet they participate in knowledge networks and communities of interest that span organizational boundaries. These networks serve as intelligent "synaptic webs" linking knowledge and ideas from the larger social system with internal expertise.

Practice Communities

Practice communities have stronger ties and more deliberate relationships than knowledge networks. In a practice community, people really want to learn from each other and find ways to create events or projects that will help all concerned improve their knowledge and skills. They may share tools, methods, and tips and may even have a systematic way of collecting these. There is a strong sense of community and a natural evolution of the group through identifiable stages.

Membership is usually self-selecting and people are held together by passion and commitment. Practice communities require a sense of mission—there is something people want to accomplish or do together that arises from their shared understanding.

Supporting Communities of Practice

Knowledge networks already exist in most organizations. The first step is not to create them but to simply find them and then make them visible to themselves and to the rest of the organization. A number of companies, however, are taking this a step further. They are looking at the naturally occurring practice communities and finding ways to work with them as more deliberate learning communities.

A community of practice is a group or network of individuals who share a concern, a set of problems, or a passion about a topic and who deepen their knowledge and expertise in this area by interacting with each other on an ongoing basis.[3] The term was coined by Etienne Wenger and Jean Lave, who were pioneer researchers in the field.[4]

Richard McDermott, who has guided the development of communities of practice in a number of global companies, points out that these networks—nesting within other networks within other networks—are a fractal type of structure of organization, where each part reflects the principles of the whole.[5] Another term for this nesting characteristic is holonomy, which comes from life sciences. Again, we are seeing the characteristics and qualities of living systems become more and more applicable to life in organizations.

SOCIAL NETWORK ANALYSIS

Social network analysis is an excellent and well-proven methodology to surface patterns of interaction and make knowledge networks visible. Figures 8.1, 8.2, and 8.3 show how this works.

Figure 8.1 shows five workgroups, the formal reporting structure, and the people within those workgroups. It also depicts other people outside the workgroups that they interact with, such as vendors, customers, and other departments in the company. The manager in the center of the diagram would appear to be a bottleneck.

Figure 8.2 shows who each person *really* talks to and the informal networked pattern of interactions. Here, the social network analysis shows that for the most part the interactions follow the formal reporting structure, with only limited direct interaction between the five groups. More frequent interactions are indicated with heavier lines, and dotted lines are interactions that could not be confirmed but are probably there.

In this situation, a new manager was brought in who wanted to move toward a more distributed workflow. One year later a second analysis was completed, showing the groups interacting much more with each other. Almost everyone has more points of interaction, the network pathways have been considerably altered, and the manager is no longer a bottleneck (see Figure 8.3).

IMPROVING SHARING IN A KNOWLEDGE NETWORK

One of the strategies employed by people who deliberately use network dynamics is to seek out opportunities to connect communities and groups that are not yet connected. Such places are called structural holes. When a node comes into place spanning such a hole, that node

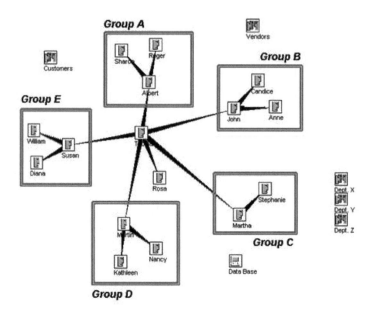

FIGURE 8.1   *Formal reporting structure, which would show up on the organization chart.* (*Courtesy Valdis Krebs.*)[6]

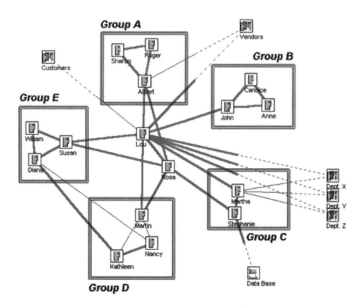

FIGURE 8.2   *Social network analysis of who people actually talk with in the course of their work.* (*Courtesy Valdis Krebs.*)[7]

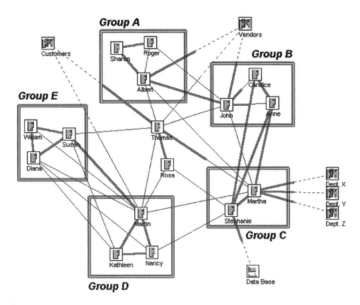

FIGURE 8.3   *Social network analysis of the same group one year later, after moving to a more distributed workflow. (Courtesy Valdis Krebs.)*[8]

receives a diverse combination of information and knowledge that is not available to anyone else in the network. This is one of those in-between places where innovation can emerge. Just the addition of a single node and the appropriate connections can dramatically improve network benefits. Working with these network patterns can create a competitive advantage that is extremely difficult for a competitor to duplicate.

From the vantage point of an individual, it is not too hard to see what is happening two steps out, with one's own direct contacts and their direct contacts. By three steps out, the connections begin to get fuzzy and it can be difficult to have a clear idea of what is happening in the rest of the network. If the knowledge or expert you happen to need is in another part of the network, say a cluster or two away, then the number of people you need to go through and the length of the pathway to connect to what you need become critical.

One strategy to reduce the length of the pathways is to add cross-network links. Just a few randomly added links can improve a network's path significantly. Very small adjustments can cause large positive changes. One way companies have been adding random links is to create directories of people with certain types of expertise. The directories provide links with available people who can be contacted directly. This can greatly reduce the number of network connections to go through.

Another key pattern is how tightly or loosely different parts of the network are connected. According to complexity theory, systems that adapt best are those that are only partially connected. Too much connection or interdependency locks up movement; too little connectivity and the system dissipates. Shona Brown and Kathleen Eisenhart use the analogy of traffic lights. If there are too few there is chaos. Too many results in gridlock. A moderate number of connections creates structure while allowing drivers to adapt their routes to traffic conditions.[9]

In order to maximize network benefits, it is important to obtain wide network reach without having too many direct ties. Research has shown that both individuals and groups that are central in organizational networks, yet are not overwhelmed by direct ties, are very effective in getting things done. Those burdened with too many direct ties are not as effective.[10]

Tracing knowledge artifacts

It is also possible to use social network analysis to trace the evolution and usage of a particular knowledge artifact. An artifact is something created for a practical purpose. In a work environment, a knowledge artifact might be a document, a body of source code for a software program, an engineering schematic, or a template for a proposal. Even a process is an artifact.

Using social network analysis, Valdis Krebs and Charles Armstrong, CEO of S.A. Armstrong Ltd., came up with a way to identify which particular knowledge artifacts people in the knowledge network share or work on together. By the time a particular artifact, say a proposal template, is passed along from one person to another several times, it may be considerably modified from its original version. The analysis provides a way to trace the development of new knowledge and identify some of the most critical people involved in innovation and knowledge creation.[11]

Artifacts themselves can serve as ties in the network. Two people may not have a tie through their personal contacts, but might share the same knowledge artifacts. Those artifacts then can become connectors for two people who may not otherwise cross paths.

Contrast this dynamic view of how an artifact moves with the usage data generated on the Eureka best practice database discussed in Chapter 7. The Eureka database can track the users of a particular item, and it shows its originators. It does not show the pathway that the solution may take as it is diffused and replicated across the technicians' group. While that may not be important for service tips, it could be critical in new product development, product launch, or engineering design work.

The pathways and connecters of artifacts and their offspring have a close correlation to the social ties between people. By utilizing both views it becomes possible to identify not only the knowledge networks but also the artifact networks. This allows people to become more aware of their own knowledge creation and usage pattern, and to be more deliberate about knowledge reuse.

BENEFITS OF COMMUNITIES OF PRACTICE

With today's increasingly mobile workforce, people are often more aligned to their professional identity than to their organizational affiliation. For this reason, companies such as American Management Services, that actively connect new hires to practice communities, find that retention levels increase dramatically.

Healthy and active communities of practice bring a number of business benefits.

For the business, they:

- Help drive strategy
- Support faster problem solving both locally and organization wide
- Speed customer response
- Aid in developing, recruiting, and retaining talent
- Build core capabilities and knowledge competencies
- More rapidly diffuse practices for operational excellence
- Cross-fertilize ideas and increase opportunities for innovation
- Reduce rework and needless redundancy
- Spawn new ideas for products and services

For the community of practice, they:

- Help build common language, methods, and models around specific competencies
- Embed knowledge and expertise in a larger population
- Aid retention of knowledge when employees leave the company
- Increase access to expertise across the company
- Provide a means to share power and influence with the formal parts of the organization

For the individual, they:

- Decrease the learning curve
- Help people do their jobs
- Provide a stable sense of community with internal colleagues and with the company
- Foster a learning-focused sense of identity
- Help develop individual skills and competencies
- Help a knowledge worker stay current
- Provide challenges and opportunities to contribute

Who is Using Communities of Practice?

Many other terms are used in corporations to describe similar groups of people. BPAMOCO refers to these as enabling networks. At Montgomery Watson Harza, they are knowledge communities[13] Others may refer to them as learning communities or practice communities.

Xerox is an old hand at communities, having supported research at the Institute for Research in Learning in the 1980s. Today, communities of practice are deeply embedded in Xerox culture.

Shell encourages "dual citizenship," whereby everyone is a member of their functional workgroup and an active participant in at least one knowledge sharing network. This helps spread learning from projects more widely across the company.

Other companies leveraging communities of practice include Johnson & Johnson, General Motors, Ford Motors, Pillsbury, The World Bank, The Veterans Administration, Hewlett-Packard, Chevron, Raytheon, Shell Oil, the large consulting groups, Samsung Life, Philip Morris, Daimler-Chrylser, IBM, Intel, Lucent Technologies, and Motorola.

How Communities of Practice Are Different

Communities of practice emerge in the social space between project teams and knowledge networks. A loosely organized knowledge network of people who share common interests can gel into a focused community when people recognize new, shared opportunities or begin to seek a significant breakthrough. From the other direction, multiple project teams engaged in similar tasks and needing to share what they know will often evolve into real learning communities.

Communities of practice are also distinctly different from teams. Team skills cannot simply be transferred to communities of practice.

There are important differences that require different approaches. In work teams and project teams, managers generally predetermine major goals and the basic nature of the joint enterprise. In a real community of practice, these are negotiated among members. Further, a community life cycle is determined by the value it creates for its *members*, not by project deadlines.

Also, where membership in workgroups and project teams is usually assigned or selected by the leader, a community of practice is usually self-selecting. Communities are defined by *knowledge* rather than task. People participate because they personally identify with the topic and enterprise of the community. Melissie Rumizen has worked with community of practice development at both the National Securities Administration and Buckman Laboratories. "I had to learn," she says, "that these learning communities are more like volunteer organizations. They simply cannot be managed like a project or team." A community continually redefines itself and its enterprise in a more emergent, organic way.

KEY ELEMENTS

Etienne Wenger, Richard McDermott, and Bill Snyder describe three important elements of communities of practice.[14] To be considered a real community of practice all three elements must be present.

1. *Domain (what they know)*. People organize around a domain of knowledge that gives members a sense of joint enterprise and brings them together. Members identify with the domain of knowledge and a joint undertaking that emerges from shared understanding of their situation.

2. *Community (who they are)*. People function as a *community* through relationships of mutual engagement that bind members together into a social entity. They interact regularly and engage in joint activities that build relationships and trust.

3. *Practice (what they do).* The community builds capability in
    its practice by developing shared repertoires and resources—
    tools, documents, routines, vocabulary, symbols, artifacts, etc.
    —that embody the accumulated knowledge of the community.
    This accumulated knowledge serves as a foundation for future
    learning.

SUPPORTING PRACTICE COMMUNITIES

For companies, working with communities and knowledge networks
is different from working with project teams or intact working
groups. However, there are many ways in which communities can be
supported.

One way to think about support is in terms of roles that people play.
If a company is serious about supporting communities of practice, it
needs to help people define personal and collective roles and responsibilities so that communities are not just "one more thing to do," but
simply the way people do their work.

Most of all, people need time, space, and budgets to meet and collaborate. Learning communities are a big draw to new hires, and they
can affect recruitment practices, job rotation, and career development
processes. This means reward systems, recognition, job definitions,
and relationships will change across the entire organization. Even
though practice communities are more informal than workgroups or
business units, they still are purposeful groups of people.

One of the features of a real community is that it largely self-
organizes. However, workplace communities are also serving a business purpose and need a level of structure and support that will enable
them to be effective. There are new roles to be defined for community
champions, members, experts, mentors, organizers, coordinators,
communicators, facilitators, and support staff. Membership is usually
open to anyone who has an interest. While it is important that people
largely self-select for the roles they play, it is critical to ensure that there

is a corporate champion to provide resources and help the community have influence.

Dan Holtshouse, corporate strategy director at Xerox, suggests that one important area of support is helping communities find ways to share power and influence with the formal parts of the organization. "Having forums, platforms, etc., for the voice of the community to be heard as a part of the business processes is something we in business need to do much better." So not only do individual roles need to be revamped, but the role of the community itself needs to be negotiated. The roles a community can play range from informal, even hidden, to those that are more formally supported. There is an art to this though —going too far can institutionalize them to the degree people actually stop learning.

Supporting a Community through its Life Cycle[15]

Etienne Wenger has worked with colleagues Richard McDermott and Bill Snyder to define five stages of development in communities of practice.[16] Although the following is not by any means a complete list of activities, it illustrates some of the ways practice communities can be supported in different stages of their life cycle.[12]

Stage 1: Potential

At this stage there is a loose network of people with similar issues and needs. People need to find each other, discover common ground, and prepare for a community. Opportunities for support include:

- Staging an awareness campaign and identifying benefits of practice communities
- Diagnosing infrastructure issues concerning communities
- Leading creation of a corporate community development strategy
- Identifying which communities to support

- Helping people find common ground through interviews and group dialogue
- Identifying what knowledge a community wants or needs to share
- Coaching community champions

Stage 2: Coalescing

At this stage people come together and launch a community. People find value in engaging in learning activities and designing a community. Opportunities for support include:

- Facilitating dialogue around identity and joint enterprise
- Designing, facilitating, and documenting informal meetings
- Mapping knowledge flows and knowledge relationships
- Designing and creating a community support structure
- Coaching community coordinators, communicators, and support staff
- Working with designers of workspaces to improve knowledge sharing
- Building organizational support

Stage 3: Maturing

The community takes charge of its practice and grows. Members set standards, define a learning agenda, and deal with growth. By now they are engaging in joint activities, creating artifacts, and developing commitment and relationships. Opportunities for support include:

- Guiding a community through growth
- Codeveloping support strategies for the group learning agenda
- Creating frameworks, guidelines, measures, and reality checks for development
- Designing knowledge capture and documentation systems

- Designing, convening, and facilitating conferences
- Working with the community on issues around relationships
- Building a community of coordinators to share best practices on community building

Stage 4: Stewardship

The community is established and goes through cycles of activities. Its members need ways to sustain energy, renew interest, educate novices, find a voice, and gain influence. Opportunities for support include:

- Working with the community on commitment and sustaining energy
- Addressing organizational issues that may be helping or hindering activity
- Linking community learning to individual career development goals
- Helping negotiate the role of the community in organizational decision making
- Forging linkages with other groups and communities for mutual learning

Stage 5: Transformation

The community has outlived its usefulness and people move on. The challenges are about letting go, defining a legacy, and keeping in touch. Opportunities for support include:

- Helping people let go
- Facilitating storytelling
- Preserving artifacts, memorabilia, and history
- Convening reunions
- Maintaining maps and directories

The Knowledge Environment

Knowledge networks and communities cannot grow where there is no trust. As companies move focus more on people and less on processes and systems, the supporting conditions and culture become ever more critical.

Companies that create an environment of trust with strong social connections and knowledge sharing are finding their culture to be a source of real competitive advantage. Levering and Moskowitz's list of 100 best companies to work for shows those companies that have a people friendly work culture consistently enjoy higher valuation and profitability.[18]

Culture change is a very broad issue and cannot be addressed in a paragraph or two. There is a great deal of management literature and practice devoted to understanding and changing organizational culture. No one really changes a culture directly, of course, but cultures do shift when different behaviors are taught, coached, supported, and rewarded. Any company serious about supporting knowledge sharing must add working in deliberate ways with environment and culture to the skill set for leaders and managers.

Learning Together

With all the recent emphasis on networks, communities, virtual teams, and collaboration during the past few years, managers have been inundated with the message that we are moving to a new level of social connection in business. Emotional intelligence has been recognized as a quality that has value in the workplace. People are being encouraged to form cohesive workgroups, collaborate, and appreciate each other's talents.

With all that, we have made great strides in making work more enjoyable and creative. We lose our way from time to time when recessionary pressures increase stress and workloads. But for the most part, the trend is toward building not just working relationships, but also human relationships that build trust and open the channels for knowledge sharing and creativity.

While we have learned to collaborate, we still have much to learn about the dynamics of group creativity and deeper learning. In Chapter 9 we will explore where we are in our collaborative capacity, what lies before us as we better understand the complex systems we are a part of, and what tools and methods will help us move forward.

CHAPTER ENDNOTES

[1] Rob Cross, "More than an Answer: How Seeking Information Facilitates Knowledge Creation and Use," IBM Institute of Knowledge Management, September 2000.

[2] Valdis Krebs, "Managing Core Competencies of the Corporation," The Advisory Board Company, 1996. Available at www.orgnet.com.

[3] Etienne Wenger, Richard McDermott, and William M Snyder, *Cultivating Communities of Practice: A Guide to Managing Knowledge,* Harvard Business School Press, 2002.

[4] Jean Lave and Etienne Wenger, *Situated Learning: Legitimate Peripheral Participation,* Cambridge University Press, 1991.

[5] Etienne Wenger, Richard McDermott, and William M Snyder, *Cultivating Communities of Practice: A Guide to Managing Knowledge.*

[6] Valdis Krebs, "Managing Core Competencies of the Corporation," The Advisory Board Company, 1996. Available at www.orgnet.com.

[7] Valdis Krebs, "Managing Core Competencies of the Corporation."

[8] Valdis Krebs, "Managing Core Competencies of the Corporation."

[9] Shona L Brown and Kathleen M Eisenhardt, *Competing on the Edge: Strategy as Structured Chaos,* Harvard Business School Press, 2001.

[10] Rob Cross, Nitin Norhia, and Andrew Parker, "Six Myths About Informal Networks and How to Overcome Them," *MIT Sloan Management Review,* Spring 2002.

[11] Charles Armstrong and Valdis Krebs, "Knowledge Networks: We are our Artefacts (sic)," *HIRIM Journal,* October–December 2000.

[12] Verna Allee, "Knowledge Networks and Communities of Practice," *Organizational Development Practitioner,* Fall–Winter, 2000. Eric Lesser and John Storch, "Communities of Practice and Organizational Performance," *IBM Systems Journal,* vol. 40, no. 4, 2001.

[13] Richard McDermott, and Vic Gulas, "Knowledge Communities at Montgomery Watson Harza," presentation for Braintrust Conference, February 2002.

[14] Etienne Wenger, Richard McDermott, and William M Snyder, *Cultivating Communities of Practice: A Guide to Managing Knowledge.*

[15] Verna Allee, "Knowledge Networks and Communities of Practice."

[16] Etienne Wenger, "Communities of Practice: Stewarding Knowledge," November, 1999. Article available through the author at www.wenger.com.

[17] Etienne Wenger, "Communities of Practice: Stewarding Knowledge."

[18] R. Levering and M. Moskowitz, "The 100 Best Companies to Work For" *Fortune*, January 10, 2000.

Knowledge cannot be separated from the human networks and communities that create it, use it, and transform it.

NINE
Communal Learning and Beyond

Organizational cognition or intelligence is very complex. When we explore social processes of learning, sense making, and knowledge creation in organizations, we are addressing the cognitive aspect of a living system, as we first noted in Chapter 4.

As individuals mature they are able to move to more advanced levels of abstract reasoning. They also learn to work with their inner lives of emotions, feelings, perceptions, assumptions, and beliefs. Self-mastery is deeply related to our capacity for coherence in our experience, thought, and action.

Organizational intelligence also has a maturing process. Some organizations collectively work at a higher level of reflection and personal mastery than others. Those that have actively worked to develop learning capability feel they are able to adapt faster and more effectively to changes in their environment. This chapter looks at how advanced cognitive capacities develop, and how collectively we can know ourselves better and be more conscious in our actions.

COMMUNAL LEARNING

Most group work and collaboration in organizations, even that of communities of practice, is based on communal learning.[1] This mode of learning is about understanding context, relationships, and trends in order to understand what promotes or impedes effectiveness. It involves the making of meaning in the context of the work that people do. In learning theory this would be double-loop learning. Double-loop learning is the ability to reflect on one's actions, choose alternatives, and modify one's behavior. This means people can detect and correct errors, choose alternative paths to reach a goal, and modify norms, policies, and objectives as needed.[2]

Taking effective action together requires extensive socialization and conversation, but that does not mean the group's members will extend their learning to the next level and reflect on the learning process itself. People may reason together, but they rarely reflect on their deeper assumptions or question the way they reach their conclusions. Most of our work together on projects and teams would be typical of this model of learning.

In Chapter 7, I talked about sharing best practices across work-groups. Best practice sharing is a good example of a communal learning process. Other examples of the double-loop learning process are the Action Review and storytelling.

The Action Review

Action Reviews are an excellent communal learning tool. Many companies are now making them a regular part of the way people do their work.

The Action Review is a simple team learning process that is held at critical milestones during a project. They are a way for people to learn immediately from their activities. Action Reviews are a major cornerstone of BPAMACO's successful knowledge initiative (modeled after the U.S. Army Action Review) which was developed in 1985, and have been adopted throughout the company.[3]

An Action Review asks four basic questions:[4]

1.   What was supposed to happen?
2.   What actually happened?
3.   What worked well?
4.   What did not work well?

This simple review helps people reflect on what they were trying to do, notice differences and alternatives, and learn from their experiences. Ideally, people select someone to be the facilitator to be sure everyone is heard, and learning is noted in a way that can be shared with others. The review can be an informal fifteen minutes or larger and more structured reviews during large projects.

Storytelling

The most natural and effective vehicle for communal learning is "the story." A hypertext software developer once observed that the universe is not really composed of atoms, it is composed of stories. Stories work at multiple levels and serve many purposes. They provide the context of all our daily activity, help orient new hires to enterprise history and values, and define desirable or undesirable behaviors. We all participate in the collaborative myth making of our company, just as we live our own individual story. Stories are so powerful that knowledge management experts, such as Stephen Denning of the World Bank and Dave Snowden of the IBM Institute for Knowledge Management, have undertaken research to help people learn this powerful "analogue" approach to creating and sharing context.[5]

We indoctrinate people into any culture by telling tales. Southwest Airlines is a great example of a company in which the outrageous and humorous stories people tell form the backbone of customer service. President Steve Keller is one of the most colorful CEOs in American business, and a superb manager of meaning. He sets the tone of the culture by spinning yarns of company heroes, including himself, as an example of desirable behavior. The constant telling and retelling of tales of outrageous customer service efforts foster a culture of empowerment and friendliness.

The only way we know we have learned anything is when our story changes. People learn best when they get to do something and then *talk* about it, telling the story of what they just did, so that what they "learned" becomes a new story, a new language. People know learning took place because they themselves told something new and insight-ful—for them.

Learning processes such as Action Reviews, benchmarking, storytel-ling, and best practice sharing are appropriate and useful for most of our everyday projects and work activities. However, when our actions might affect other parts of the organization, our customers, our suppli-ers, or our business network partners, then we need a different type of learning approach. In the learning experiences just described, the point of reference for learning is past experience.

Before we can truly begin sensing how the future is unfolding, we must move to another starting point. The time horizon of attention only encompasses the immediate past, the present, and the immediate future. We must be able to sense and learn our way into a future that has not yet emerged.

Our starting point cannot be the past, but must be the fully informed and aware present. This requires developing the capacity for what Gregory Bateson refers to as *deutero learning*.[6] Now that is a very big term for what is basically a simple idea. It refers to second-order learning—that is, the capacity to reflect on and inquire into pre-vious contexts for learning. In other words, thinking and learning systemically.

Deutero learning questions the context by considering all the sys-temic factors concerning a particular action. It considers the historic forces that led to an action, the full systemic implications of that action in the present context, and the future implications of that action in the unfolding future. It therefore goes considerably beyond communal learning, which interprets and translates only the most immediate con-text. It takes the device of the story and projects it into the future by exploring possibilities.

Deutero learning is the foundation for true systems thinking. It is the learning mode that seeks to understand dynamic relationships and nonlinear processes, discerning the patterns that connect. It is learning that recognizes the embeddedness and interdependence of systems, enabling us to work with complexity and network dynamics.

Deutero learning, which I prefer to call systemic learning, also means inquiring into our thinking processes. It seeks out patterns of logic, surfacing and challenging assumptions and beliefs. Doing this well takes practice, but is typical of advanced systemic thinking.

Tools for Whole-System Learning

We have made great strides toward whole-system thinking by introducing a number of new tools and processes into the workplace. During the late 1980s and early 1990s, a number of whole-system learning approaches began to surface. These include large-scale collaborative processes that "get the whole system in the room."

Other helpful tools are meeting facilitation methods that are supported with templates or graphic facilitation to guide whole-system thinking. Analytical tools such as system dynamics, popularized by Peter Senge as a management discipline, have now been introduced to a wider managerial audience as a way to see whole-system patterns. Here are two examples of group learning tools that support systemic learning.

Large-Scale Collaboration

One of the best-known processes is the large-scale collaborative change method pioneered by Kathy Dannemiller.[7] In this approach, as many as three hundred people may be brought together in one large room over a one- to two-day period. Through a structured, facilitated process people work through a complex change issue together. The process scales to any size group by having people work in small groups and by using templates for structuring the content of their contributions.

Prior to large-group processes, planning for change was always accomplished by a few high-level people and then the change was "rolled out" to the rest of the organization. Such efforts are really more like "roll overs." Management just rolls over people's concerns and pushes the change effort through. People sort of duck down while it all rolls over them, and then they pop back up and do the same things they have always done.

Large-scale collaborative processes take an entirely different view of how to work with a complex system. Working from the philosophy that no one group of people can understand a real system, the goal is to find a way to have the whole system reflect on its behaviors and change itself. First, get the whole system in the room to address the issues. The whole system is either literally represented by having every employee of a company or division participate, or by including a significant number of representatives from every level and area of responsibility. GE's famous workouts and town hall meetings are examples of this large-scale collaborative approach.

This type of change approach has proven to be enormously effective. The session is a powerful way to get everybody "on the same page" and aligned toward a common purpose. By surfacing all the concerns and issues in the beginning, people feel included in the process and are more willing to support the effort. The plans that emerge from the collective understanding are usually much more workable than ones developed by only a few.

Graphic Meeting Facilitation

At the same time that large-scale collaborative processes became popular, meeting facilitation took a new turn. Thanks in large part to the talent and leadership of David Sibbet, founder of Grove Consulting, people found that skillful use of graphics during meetings could help people discover systemic insights and patterns. At first people simply graphically depicted the themes and issues that were being surfaced, telling the story of the group and its learning process. Gradually the visual aspect of collaborative work has been taking on more importance as a way for people to actively reflect and create meaning together. Graphic recording has evolved to graphic facilitation.

Sibbet has identified a number of collaborative processes that people engage in repeatedly in the workplace. One of his newest contributions to the field is the development of a number of templates that support project teams in thinking systemically. An example is shown in Figures 9.1 and 9.2.

The first drawing, Figure 9.1, is an example of a graphic template, which is usually displayed as a large banner on the wall of a meeting room. Using the template ensures that people have addressed systemic issues and concerns regarding their project. Figure 9.2 shows the same template as completed by a group.

The Challenge of Reflection

The methods described here represent a good beginning for seeing and comprehending a larger present from a more systemic viewpoint. It is the type of thinking that is essential for working with network patterns and dynamics, and it is the new platform from which we can learn to

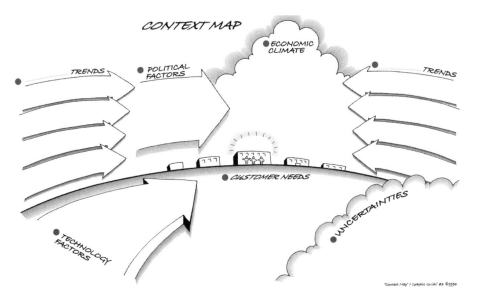

FIGURE 9.1 *Graphic template for guiding a discussion that includes systemic issues. (Courtesy Grove Consulting.)*

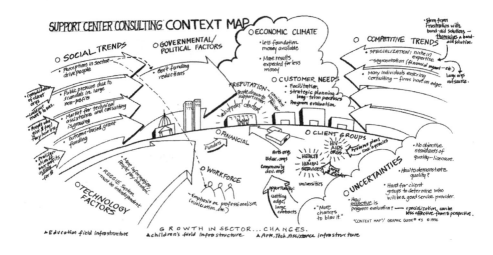

FIGURE 9.2   *The template as completed by a work group. (Courtesy Grove Consulting.)*

sense future opportunities. However, systemic thinking must be combined with a deeper level of reflective learning that taps into our inner resources and wisdom.

Moving to a deeper level of reflection in a business setting can be a challenge. Some cultures, such as that in the U.S., are so task-driven and action-oriented that pausing to reflect feels odd or perhaps even like time wasted. However, once groups begin to develop the capacity for true reflective learning they find that it is the real efficiency factor for taking effective action. Taking time out for reflection is widely accepted on an individual level. It is a legitimate part of business decision making as well.

GENERATIVE LEARNING

True reflection opens the possibility for *generative learning*. This term was introduced by learning organization advocate Peter Senge.

For Senge, generative learning is learning that enhances our capacity to create.[8] It is value-driven learning that seeks what is alive, compelling, and energizing. It heeds the call for renewal and expresses a willingness to see radical possibilities beyond the boundaries of current thinking.

Generative learning requires heuristic, open-ended explorations and creative processes. It allows for the discovery of one's highest capabilities, talents, aspirations, and passion. Renewal and new possibilities open when people touch the deepest core of purpose and values that shape the enterprise.

Some large-scale group processes, used skillfully, can lend themselves to this type of exploration. Marvin Weisborg devised a more generative, forward-looking process called *Future Search*, that is a facilitated large-group process[9] The methodology uses specific whole-system questions that guide a group through visiting their history, analyzing their present situation, and looking forward into their desired future. It helps people step back, review, and envision their unfolding story.

Another method, *Open Space Technology* devised by Harrison Owen, has introduced many people to a simple way to surface the learning questions that are most alive for a group of people. This facilitated process uses simple organizing principles for people to find the questions and issues that matter most to the group, and to structure learning conversations around them.[10]

As we begin to develop the capacity for whole-system thinking and generative learning, we find we must bring more of ourselves to the process. Complex systems are a world of paradox. We must learn to deal with possibilities instead of probabilities. Much of what we need to understand cannot be grasped by trying to figure things out with our heads alone. We must learn the "good sensing" that helps us understand what is emerging and how we need to work with it. For that, we must draw on our full range of intelligence and wisdom as sensory, emotive, and thinking human beings.

The Game of Business As Described by W. Brian Arthur[11]

Imagine you are milling about in a large casino with the top figures in high tech—the Gateses, Gerstners, and Groves of their industries. Over at one table, a game is starting called Multimedia. Over at another is a game called Web Services. In the corner is Electronic Banking. There are many such tables. You sit at one.

"How much to play?" you ask.
"Three billion," the croupier replies.
"Who'll be playing?" you ask.
"We won't know until they show up," he replies.
"What are the rules?"
"Those will emerge as the game unfolds," says the croupier.
"What are my odds of winning?" you wonder.
"We can't say," responds the house. "Do you still want to play?"

—W. Brian Arthur

Collective Knowing

Most business learning experiences are about learning from the past. We are now seeking ways that we might learn into the future. A number of thoughtful researchers are considering how we might experience a larger collective knowing that will help us sense what is happening, make meaning of it together, and choose paths of action that lead us to a more compelling, life-affirming, and energizing future.[12]

In *The Knowledge Evolution*, I made the point that everything we create, including our organizations, is a creative expression of our minds, our sense of who we are, and our intentions. As we move to a more complex, interconnected world, we are most truly challenged to develop the inner technologies of mind that shape our social systems, our relationships, the businesses we create—and in a very real sense, the world we live in.

Recently a group of respected thinkers engaged in a series of conversations and dialogues around organizational knowledge, learning, and leadership. Participants included Brian Arthur, Ikujiro Nonaka, Peter Senge, Joe Jaworski, Otto Scharmer, Aries de Geus, Eleanor Rosch, and Fransisco Varela. It would be difficult to find a more distinguished group of thinkers, researchers, and commentators on organizations and management practices. The overwhelming consensus of the group is that awareness of how we create our shared social reality is the most important aspect of business life we will need to learn for a successful future.

Let's take a closer look at how knowledge happens. How do we create our shared social reality, our collective knowledge?

"Sensing" Our World

There is an ancient saying, that one can never step into the same river twice. The river is always different. Even if the rocks are in the same place, there are variations in the water flow and the whirlpools and eddies. They may be in the same place they were the year before, but there will be variations in the currents. The dynamics will be the same, but the exact way the funnel of the whirlpool bends and turns will be different. The water is never the same water. The water one stepped into a year ago has long since poured into the sea, diffusing through the ocean currents, eventually evaporating to form the clouds. Even the experience will be different; the light and cloud cover may be different, or the air could be a little cooler.

We also never experience the same knowledge twice. We can express similar ideas using a wide variety of sentence structures, but the message is modified and changed according to the person we are talking with. If we pay close attention we realize that even our ideas are fluid in conversation, subtly shaping themselves around the other thoughts in the conversation space, drawing on different analogies, emphasizing different aspects.

We are in a constant, collective journey of storytelling, sense making, and creation. Knowledge is a conversation. It is not a static "thing," but a continual process in motion, emerging in the shared communal learning space that arises between people. Every conversation reshapes our knowledge, modifying it to fit new circumstances, expanding it with new information or connections, pruning out ideas and expressions that are no longer useful.

Worlds of Knowledge

A colleague and friend, Sherrin Bennett, once drew a simple diagram for me that I find very useful (see Figure 9.3). Whenever there are two or more people in conversation, there are several knowledge "worlds" that are being created at once.

Both individual knowledge and shared knowledge emerge in, and only in, the conversation. What is individually offered into the conversation is created *in that moment* specifically for the purpose of that conversation. Nonverbal communication is also created in the moment, as a type of dance that happens between people.

In the creative center of the conversation, yet a different universe of knowing arises—as shared understandings or insights discovered by the participants—that is unique to that particular conversation. This creative center of knowledge is emergent, in that it could not be known or predicted prior to the conversation. Further, that shared knowledge and the other individual offerings act as influences and agents to reshape or re-create the knowledge that the individual might hold.

Even if there is no actual conversational partner at hand, there is always an imagined presence that we are communicating with. Someone writing a letter is making an offering into a conversation with another specific person. The communication is quite different whether

FIGURE 9.3   *There are multiple worlds of knowing in a single conversation, interacting in a field of coherence and meaning.*

that imagined presence is a family member, a colleague, or a friend. There may be a delay in the response or even no response, but the same dynamic of knowledge creation applies. Our own emergent knowledge is shaped by the anticipated or imagined response to what we are saying.

Thinking of knowledge as an active conversational process departs from some schools of thinking that focus only on individual perception, information processing, and thinking. I am suggesting that beyond raw sensory data, our perceptions, thinking, and communication are *all* essentially social acts and are aspects of a shared collective consciousness. If we would improve the quality of knowledge, then we must enter more deliberately and consciously into our conversations as the next level of learning and knowledge work.

CONSCIOUS CONVERSATION

Pioneers in learning organizations point out that most of our business conversations are not conversations; they are discussions. Discussion has the same root as the word *percussion*, to hit. Most meetings consist of people jockeying to have their ideas heard and arguing their positions. If we want to move to the kinds of conversations that support the needed skills of sensing and sense making, we must find new ways of being together. Yet it is rare for companies to train and coach people in how to have more meaningful dialogue or seriously address the challenges of collaborative decision making.

Juanita Brown and David Isaacs have focused on community building and change with several global companies, including Hewlett-Packard. They insist that *conversation* is a core business process, because it is through conversation that decisions get made and real work gets done.[13] As experienced facilitators, they have hosted conversations using a variety of different formats, including dialogue and graphic facilitation. Their work focuses especially on conscious conversations, those with the quality of deeper reflection that typifies generative learning.

Knowledge Café

In the mid-1990s, a group of early leaders in knowledge management and intellectual capital formed a community of practice and began meeting regularly. Members of the group included Hubert Saint-Onge, Leif Edvinsson, Myron Kellnor-Rogers, and a number of other practitioners, researchers, and consultants. When I joined the group shortly before it dispersed, I found they were using a group knowledge process they had dubbed the Knowledge Café. It is a simple methodology for holding a large conversation, one that supports the group in weaving themes and seeing larger patterns emerge. The process was born one day as the group met in Juanita Brown and David Isaac's living room, and has now been used in hundreds of different settings around the world.

There are many variations on the Café method, but some approaches are especially useful for evoking a deeper quality of learning. Partnering with colleague Nancy Marguilies, Juanita and David have fine tuned ways to visually represent emerging themes and help group members weave their collective insights into meaningful patterns that open future possibilities. Café techniques have spread so quickly and are so powerful that Juanita Brown has undertaken a serious research study of the Café experience. The project includes dozens of interviews with both facilitators and participants, and draws on her many years experience in community building, dialogue, and working with other aspects of collective intelligence.[14]

The World Café

The World Café is an intentional way to create a living network of conversations around questions that matter. One can be conducted with small groups of ten to twenty people, or can be scaled up to involve several hundred people. It is suggested that one or two people organize and facilitate the process, but that the overall feeling be casual and informal. The idea is to capture the spontaneity of a real café, but to have a more serious focus on a specific topic or issue.

People join several other people at a small café-style table or in a small conversation cluster, exploring a question of importance to their lives, work, or community. Other people are sitting in similar groupings nearby. While there are no hard and fast rules about how to do it, this process seems to work best when people engage with a question for twenty minutes or so, and then some (not all) participants move to other tables and conversations. The people who don't rotate to other tables keep the continuity of their conversation and help weave ideas.

A free Resource Guide for hosting conversations is available for download at www.theworldcafe.com.

Take-Aways from the Knowledge Café

One particularly important insight emerged from Brown's research. One of the dilemmas in trying to move people into dialogue is the tendency of people to maintain their personal positions and judgments. As a result, a group often never reaches a level of coherence, but remains fragmented into different individual viewpoints. However, the Café conversations create a much different pattern of relationship to the whole than other types of dialogue or group work.

Something unexpected happens when members are charged with the responsibility of not only putting forth their own ideas but also becoming "ambassadors of meaning" or "theme weavers" as people move from one conversation to another. They listen for and carry the collective ideas expressed in previous conversations to new Café tables. People learn to listen for other viewpoints, and not only honor those perspectives but to actually represent them to others. The resulting quality of shared listening and shared meaning is significantly higher than with other approaches.

The Café is also a metaphor for noticing how we learn, share knowledge and stories, make meaning, and co-evolve our futures through living networks of conversation. All of us move from one conversation to another, carrying the sense of the conversations with us, cross-pollinating knowledge, stories, and ideas. When we can all learn to actively play ambassadors or weavers of meaning and themes, we will develop the capacity to see the larger patterns of common understanding that help us make sense of our world.

Needing Each Other

The challenges that face all of us in becoming global citizens—and in shaping a world that works for all—are enormously complex. We need each other. We need all our talents and intelligence to make sense of what is happening around us and to move to the type of generative learning that will open new possibilities. As systems thinking pioneer Meg Wheatley tells us, "Human conversation is the most ancient and easiest way to cultivate the conditions for change—personal change, community and organizational change, planetary change.[15]

The Café experience, knowledge networks, and communities of practice all demonstrate that the pattern of knowledge also expresses the network pattern of a living system. As we learn to engage in more conscious conversations, we are developing the capacity for self-reflection, self-knowledge, and collective wisdom. As nodes in the ever-changing patterns of our organizations and business networks, we must bring all of who we are into our work, to achieve the full potential of our individual and collective intelligence and our wisdom.

CHAPTER ENDNOTES

[1] Verna Allee, *The Knowledge Evolution: Expanding Organizational Intelligence*, Butterworth-Heinemann, 1997.

[2] Gregory Bateson, *Steps to An Ecology of Mind* (New York: Ballentine, 1972).

[3] Chris Collison and Geoff Parcell, *Learning to Fly: How BP Became One of the Worlds Leading Knowledge Companies* (New York: John Wiley & Sons, 2001). Gordon R Sullivan and Michael V Harper, *Hope Is Not a Method*, Random House, 1996.

[4] Melissie Rumizen, *The Complete Idiot's Guide to Knowledge Management*, Alpha, 2001.

[5] Stephen Denning, *The Springboard: How Storytelling Ignites Action in Knowledge-Era Organizations*, Butterworth-Heinemann, 2001. Snowden, Dave, The Art and Science of Story or "Are You Sitting Comfortably?", *Business Information Review*, December 2000.

[6] Gregory Bateson, *Steps to An Ecology of Mind*.

[7] Dannemiller Tyson Associates, *Whole-Scale Change: Unleashing the Magic in Organizations*, Berrett-Koehler, 2000.

[8] Peter Senge, *The Fifth Discipline: The Art and Practice of the Learning Organization*, Currency Doubleday, 1990.

[9] Sandra Janoff and Marvin Ross Weisbord, *Future Search*, Berrett-Koehler, 2000.

[10] Harrison Owen, *Expanding our Now: The Story of Open Space Technology*, Berrett-Koehler, 1997.

[11] Joe Jaworski and C Otto Sharmer, "Leading in the Digital Economy: Sensing and Seizing Emerging Opportunities," *Dialog on Leadership*, December 2000.

[12]   A particularly thoughtful series of interviews and conversations can be found at www.dialogonleadership.org.

[13]   Juanita Brown and David Issacs, "Conversation as a Core Business Process," *The Systems Thinker*, vol. 7, no. 10, December 1996.

[14] Juanita Brown, David Isaacs, and The World Café Community, *The World Café: Living Knowledge Through Conversations that Matter*, The Systems Thinker, vol. 12, no. 5, June/July 2001. Juanita Brown, *The World Café: Living Knowledge Through Conversations that Matter*, Ph.D. dissertaton, The Fiedling Institute, 2001. Available through www.theworldcafe.com.

[15] Margaret J. Wheatley, *Turning to One Another: Simple Conversations to Restore Hope to the Future*, Berrett-Koeller, 2002.

© *2002 Hemera Technologies Inc.*

We learn, adapt, and bring forth our worlds through the network or conversations in which we participate.

—Humberto Maturana

PART IV

∽

New Strategic Perspectives and Tools

TEN

The New World of Intangibles

A living system view brings new understanding of how a business continually renews itself and creates value. These next four chapters carry the network view of the firm to the level of value creation. We will first explore the new thinking about intangibles as assets, negotiables, and deliverables. Then Chapters 12 and 13 will demonstrate a dynamic modeling technique that moves us closer to understanding business as a living system, providing a means for fine-tuning our ability to create both tangible and intangible value.

INTANGIBLES AND THE ECONOMY

Warning: you are approaching the point of no return. Once you go down the path of intangibles, you will not want to go back to your old ways of thinking about value. Very few people who have seriously delved into intangibles can squeeze back into the narrow box of financial balance sheets as indicators of either a company's real value or its potential for future success. Tom Stewart, the *Fortune* editor who first brought awareness of intangible or intellectual assets to the general public, suggests we simply drive a stake through the heart of our old accounting practices and declare them dead and buried.[1]

Some have declared digital technologies to be the new foundation of the Knowledge Economy. But technologies, as good as they are, are just enablers. The real foundation of the Knowledge Economy isn't things, it isn't bits and bytes, it isn't the balance sheet; it is people and their intelligence. However, digital technologies help people connect with each other and share images and documents to a degree and speed previously unimaginable. As a result, we have seen an explosion of sophisticated products and services that require huge amounts of intelligence, smarts, and know-how to create and deliver, but require negligible physical assets such as plants and machinery.

Nicholas Negroponte, the digital visionary who founded the Media Laboratory at MIT says: "The energy, people, spaces and vehicles needed to move physical things from country to country are suddenly a liability in an age of weightless, sizeless, colorless bits which move at the speed of light."[2]

Do intangibles actually have value? It would appear so. *CFO Magazine* now annually publishes a knowledge capital index developed and compiled by Baruch Lev, a professor at New York University. According to his calculations, companies with high levels of investment in intangibles show higher levels of knowledge earnings and far better stock performance than companies with lower levels of spending in those areas.[3]

For many managers, talking about intangibles, such as knowledge, feels like stepping off into a void. Some feel a jarring disconnect using the words *intangible* and *assets* in the same phrase. After all, accountants have strict rules for what can be called an asset, and nothing the intellectual capital crowd talks about falls into that "official" category. But that is the whole point. The most critical factors of success—the intelligence of employees, the systems and processes in place to get the work done, and the quality of customer and supplier relationships —don't show up anywhere on the balance sheet.

The Brookings Institution Task Force on Intangibles, headed by former SEC Commissioner Steven Wallman, points out that the value of any intangible asset comes from its interplay with other assets, both physical and intangible, and that attempting to value it on a stand alone basis is pointless.[4]

This is an important point. Intangibles are dynamic; they are not static like physical assets. So while some of the language of intangible

assets may be familiar, their behavior is not. Intangibles are very different. Yet the interest is continuing to increase because of a growing
understanding that financial measures cannot predict future performance. Sharon Oriel of Dow Chemical, a leader and innovator in
tracking and leveraging intellectual assets, points out: "The traditional
accounting system is focused on transactions and historical costs. To
determine the future value of a company, you don't look at past history.
You need new measures to project forward."[5]

WHAT ARE INTANGIBLES?

The terms *intangibles, intangible assets, knowledge assets,* and *intellectual
capital* are all used by different groups to describe basically the same
thing. Accountants generally use the term *intangibles,* whereas economists typically prefer *knowledge assets.* Business people generally speak
of *intellectual capital,* although the simpler term *intangibles* is gaining
ground. The premise for thinking of intangibles as assets is that knowledge, relationships, and ideas are more important for success today
than are physical assets.

An early thought leader in the field, Karl-Erik Sveiby, carefully
steers clear of the word "capital," because it suggests valuation, stock-
piling, and ownership. He encourages people to treat intangibles *as if*
they were assets, but not try to apply the traditional accounting definition of asset in a literal way. One values intangible assets, but that does
not mean enjoying ownership in the way one owns an automobile.[6]

Also, in common usage the term *asset* refers to both physical and
nonphysical attributes. We might say, "Her greatest asset is her sense
of humor." So the term asset does work well with the term intangibles.

Here is a definition of intangibles from a study by the Brookings
Institution:

> *Intangibles are nonphysical factors that contribute to or are used in
> producing goods or providing services, or that are expected to generate
> future productive benefits for the individuals or firms that control the
> use of those factors.*[7]

The short version of this would be "a nonphysical claim to future benefits." That phrase "control the use of" can be a bit slippery and misleading. Clearly, companies do not control people any more than they own them. However, a company can have considerable say over how employees use their knowledge, skills, and competence in pursuit of business objectives.

THREE TYPES OF INTANGIBLES

Let's take an example of a nonphysical asset. Think of your education. At one time you, or more likely your parents, made a considerable investment in your education. Those of you with young children are no doubt eagerly anticipating making a similar investment for them some-time in the future. So, can you show people your education? No, not the diploma—the education. Of course you can't; it is nonphysical. It is a nonphysical asset. You control its use as an asset and you would expect it to generate future productive benefits for you. So your educa-tion fits the definition above of an intangible.

Unlike physical assets though, you could not sell your education directly to someone else. You can negotiate the *use* of it in the form of a contract or as an employee, but you cannot sell or trade it for something else (like a boat) in the marketplace. So it behaves a bit differently, but it is still an asset. In business, this kind of asset falls under the category of Human Competence. Some refer to this as Human Capital, but it is rarely if ever called People Capital. A company does not control the use of people, only their competence, and that only to a limited degree.

Now consider other intangibles that help you to be successful. As a professional, you may turn some of your expertise into systems, tem-plates, or processes that help you get your work done. You have developed certain types of procedures or structures, such as your process for paying your bills or your filing system. In business, these intangible assets are referred to as Internal Structure or Structural Capital. A very small portion of these structures, documents, and processes can be legally protected in the form of patents and copyrights, but the bulk cannot because they are too generic. However, as a whole they provide an internal structure that makes it possible to deliver products and services.

You have another very valuable asset in the form of your networks and webs of business relationships, friends, colleagues, customers, and suppliers. We all have customers and suppliers, no matter what we do. If you work independently, you may have many direct customers. If you are employed by a firm, then you serve your primary customer —your employer. You also have suppliers such as banks, supply companies, printers, shippers, and others who contribute to what you produce and deliver to your customers. For a firm, these relationships provide an External Structure that allows the company to be effective in its industry and economic environment. Another common term used in this sense is Customer Capital, but that is misleading. Business relationships include suppliers, partners, and government agencies, as well as customers.

Some variation of this three-sector framework has been used fairly extensively in the intangibles arena. These focus areas were originally suggested by Karl-Erik Sveiby in the late 1980s, sparking a wide interest in intangibles in Scandinavia.[8] Among those who picked up the question was Leif Edvinsson of Skandia, a large financial services and insurance company. He holds the distinction of being appointed the first Director of Intellectual Capital. Edvinsson fine-tuned a similar but more extensive framework, The Skandia Navigator, and Skandia began publishing an Intellectual Capital Index as a complement to its annual financial report.[9] Table 10.1 explains the three sectors.

Working with Intangible Assets

Let's stay with the assumption that intangibles have value as assets. One of the ways you would manage an asset is to grow or increase it. You would also want to be sure that you are converting your assets to tangible value for the firm, that you are fully utilizing them, that they're being renewed as is appropriate, and that they are reliable and stable

TABLE 10.1   *A Common Three-Sector Framework for Intangibles*[8]

External Structure	Alliances and relationships with customers, strategic partners, suppliers, investors, and the community. Includes assets such as brand recognition and goodwill.
Human Competence	Individual and collective capabilities, knowledge, skills, experience, and problem-solving abilities that reside in people in an organization.
Internal Structure	Systems and work processes that leverage competitiveness. Includes IT, communications technologies, images, concepts and models of how the business operates as well as databases, documents, patents, copyrights, and other "codified" knowledge.

assets that will be there over time. So what is the key to increasing and leveraging intangibles? Ah, that brings us to knowledge management.

You see, the early leaders in knowledge management—Saint-Onge, Sveiby, and Edvinsson—did not start with the knowledge question; they started with intangibles. Their first question was "How is value really created?" The response they came up with was "Intangible assets are the real source of value in the knowledge economy." Then another question came up, "What is the best way to fully utilize intangibles, and how do you increase them?" So that was the second piece of the puzzle. Fortunately, most of the early practitioners talked with each other fairly frequently. Several of them put their heads together and came up with the diagram shown in Figure 10.1.

Look carefully. There are the three categories laid out in a ven diagram to indicate interdependency. There is also a dotted line labeled "Flow of Knowledge," and the word "values" is in the center. The theory goes: *a company increases and utilizes its intangible assets by creating, sharing, and leveraging **knowledge** to create economic value and enhance organizational performance.* It was felt by that early group that a company's values and purpose were the primary organizing principle,

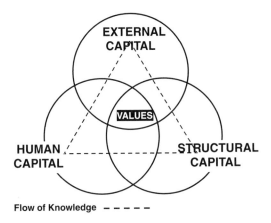

FIGURE 10.1   *A popular model of intellectual capital.*

determining who its customers are; what type of people are attracted to work there; and what type of structures and systems are required.

This simple model depicts the way the interplay of the three types of capital generates business value, as enabled by knowledge flows and a culture of learning. It captures the sense of a company in motion as it converts skills and knowledge into economic value and competitive advantage. The quality of the synergy among these three components and the ability to leverage the flow of knowledge determine a company's capacity to generate sustainable value. In this view, it is critical to manage the areas of overlap well. Human Capital should be contributing to the quality of internal structures and systems. In turn, Structural Capital should contribute to and support the improvement of Human Capital. Company values can either increase or constrict the movement and exchange of knowledge.

The Balanced Scorecard

Another popular approach for expanding organizational performance indicators is the Balanced Scorecard of Norton and Kaplan.[11] The Balanced Scorecard actually emerged in the United States at about the same time as the intellectual capital approach began to spread in north-

A Missing Link

A surprising number of people working in knowledge management are strangely unaware of this critical linkage between intangibles and the focus on knowledge. Yet, without the intangibles perspective the whole logic of knowledge management gets lost. Without an intangibles view, people engaged in knowledge initiatives find themselves in the position of having to justify their efforts only in terms of ROI. But reducing costs and gaining efficiencies is only one part of the story.

The really big value that can be realized from knowledge efforts is to increase intangible assets, such as human competence, internal structures, and business relationships. Improvements to intangibles also provide long-term gains. Value gains that show up in ROI figures tend to be only for the short term. Ideally, a knowledge undertaking would show both an immediate ROI and longer-term benefits that build capability for future value creation.

ern Europe. In this approach, four measurement categories are integrated with a company's strategy and vision: financial measures, measures for key business processes, customer measures, and learning and growth measures.

The Balanced Scorecard is based on a "building blocks" model of value creation. The foundation for success is learning and growth, which supports the execution of good business processes. The right processes ensure quality products and customer service. When customers are happy and satisfied, then financial success follows. The goal is to develop target metrics for each of the four areas. From that starting point, appropriate improvement strategies and supporting goals and activities can be developed.

The Balanced Scorecard, however, was never intended to measure intangible assets. The purpose of the scorecard is to measure and align corporate strategy. Although Norton and Kaplan used the Skandia Navigator as an example in their first book, *The Balanced Scorecard,* they did not dwell on the subject of intangibles or intellectual capital.[12] In their newer book, *The Strategy-Focused Organization,* they acknowledge that "clearly opportunities for creating value are shifting from managing tangible assets to managing knowledge-based strategies that deploy an organization's intangible assets: customer relationships, innovative products and services, high-quality and responsive operating processes, information technology and databases and employee capabilities, skills, and motivation."[13] However, they don't really go into intangibles much beyond that. In their view, a balanced scorecard that is done well would point to those intangibles that are most strategic and the knowledge activities that deserve the most attention.

What Is Wrong with This Picture?

Both the Balanced Scorecard and the Intellectual Capital approach have helped people to think about value and success from a very different vantage point than they did before. The view of enterprise that includes intangibles as assets takes us an important first step beyond industrial age management practices. It lays the foundation for understanding the dynamics of value creation in a profoundly different way.

So, what is wrong with this picture of intangibles? There is nothing seriously wrong with it as far as it goes. It just doesn't go nearly far enough. Consider the three basic categories of intangibles: human competence, internal structure, and external structure. That is still a very traditional view of the firm. It could be considered just one more variation on people, processes, and customers. Although the external structure category is steadily expanding beyond customers to include suppliers and other stakeholders, it is still limited to those who have *direct financial transactions* with the company. The role the enterprise plays in larger society and as a global citizen is completely overlooked.

This view leaves a very important block of intangibles without a seat at the table.

EXPANDING THE FRAME

Companies are located in and interact with local and global communities, acting as nodes in larger networks and systems. Enterprises affect society and the environment and in turn are dependent upon and affected by them. Healthy socioeconomic systems provide educated employees and financially successful consumers for products and services. For an unhealthy example, Silicon Valley executives are concerned because local school systems are not providing the qualified workers they need for their technology-intensive companies. Further, some employees are leaving because of the quality of life and high cost of living in the area. We cannot continue to view the larger social system as being disconnected from everyday business concerns. How can any business thrive if the global quality of life is so poor that most of the world's population faces a daily struggle for food and clean drinking water?

We have traditionally viewed environmental concerns as unrelated to our business models, other than the costs and restrictions inflicted by regulatory bodies. Business certainly doesn't hesitate to enjoy benefits such as cheap natural resources that someone else seems to bear the cost of. There are relatively small financial consequences for polluting air or water or creating toxic waste dumps. Many companies choose to pay environmental fines rather than clean up their act, because financially it makes better sense for them. So there are no real incentives to be environmentally responsible.

The health of the environment is an unrealistic blind spot in our business and economic models. How can a pharmaceutical company not be concerned with biodiversity? How can any company afford to ignore the number of purchase decisions that are informed by their environmental responsibility as a company? Young people especially are shaping their buying habits according to whether a company is one of the "good guys."

Consider the number of people who changed their buying habits after the Exxon Valdez oil spill. The accident was bad enough, but the company's slowness to respond and its uncaring attitude toward the cleanup was completely unacceptable to a large number of people. They began giving their business to companies more proactive about environmental responsibility, such as BPAMACO and Shell. Contrast Exxon's response with Johnson & Johnson's speedy recovery after the Tylenol tampering incidents in the 1980s, in which the company acted ethically and responsibly.

Companies are finding that socially responsible and "green" business practices equate to a more positive regard for their brand. This can have big economic consequences, ranging from increased sales to community acceptance when building new plants.

At the macro-economic level, there are similar issues about how assets are viewed. For example, the environment is still referred to as natural resources and is calculated in terms of board feet of lumber and mineral reserves. There is no place for a healthy ecosystem—or even clean air and water—to show up on the national accounts. Of course, for over two decades people like Hazel Henderson[14] have been advocating national accounts that include quality-of-life indicators. Only recently have people begun to respond to that call.

An Example of Expanded Intangibles

There are strong indicators that an expanded view of intangibles is already being put into play in business. There is a growing number of assessment tools such as the Deloitte & Touche Corporate Environmental Report Score Card,[15] and the Future 500 Performance Tool Kit.[16] One of the most interesting examples of the new scorecards is the recent shift of focus for Shell. Since 1999, the annual Shell Report for Royal Dutch Shell Group has emphasized its "triple bottom line" view of success: financial success, social success, and environmental success. Chairman Mark Moody-Stuart says, "Being trusted to meet societal expectations is essential for long-term profitability. We are committed to transparency, and to developing and integrating our reporting."[7]

Shell has developed a set of performance indicators that include not only financial metrics but also measures for health and safety, emissions targets and goals achieved, replanted areas, screening of suppliers, and accidents. They publicly report those metrics as well as social responsibility measures related to diversity and equal opportunity, working hours and wages, compliance with business principles (including zero bribes policy), security incidents, and compliance with age and child labor laws.

A Whole-System View of Value

The great hope and opportunity offered by the intangibles perspective is that at long last we may be able to reconcile our business and economic models with the fabric of society and the web of life. However, the opportunity requires expanding the possible domains of value to include social and environmental categories, in addition to the three common sectors used in most intangible models (see Figure 10.2). The arrows in the diagram indicate that all the domains of value act in dynamic and interdependent ways to create value for both the business and for the larger economic, social, and environmental ecosystems that any firm is part of. The other elements are defined in the list accompanying the figure.

- *Business relationships*—Alliances and business relationships with customers, strategic partners, suppliers, investors, regulatory bodies, and government groups.
- *Internal structure*—Systems and work processes that leverage competitiveness, including IT, communications technologies, systems and software, databases, documents, images, concepts and models of how the business operates, patents, copyrights, and other codified knowledge.
- *Human competence*—Individual capabilities, knowledge, skills, experience, and problem solving abilities that reside in people.

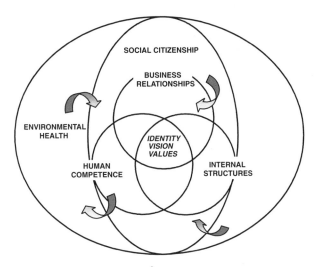

FIGURE 10.2 *A whole-system view of value.*[18] 1998 Verna Allee.

- *Social citizenship*—The quality and value of relationships enjoyed with the larger society through the exercise of corporate citizenship as a member of local, regional, and global communities.
- *Environmental health*—The value of a firm's relationship with the earth and its resources, as understood through calculation of the true costs of resources consumed by an enterprise or economy, and by determination of equitable exchange or contribution to the health and sustainability of the environment.
- *Corporate identity*—The value of a firm's vision, purpose, values, ethical stance, and leadership, as it contributes to brand equity and economic success in business and employee relationships.

Without an expanded view of intangibles, it is difficult for people to see how these ideas are really new or different. Since many people working with these ideas aren't really coming from a living system perspective, they mistakenly are trying to affix a valuation on intellectual assets, which is completely missing the point. The larger view is important for us to be able to understand exactly how organizations in general are evolving and changing.

Social Capital

Another intangible term that is entering popular usage is *social capital.* The term "social capital" has been around since the early 1900s in the field of sociology. However, until recently it has been used mostly in reference to individuals or communities, neighborhoods, cities, regions, and nation states. The World Bank defines social capital as "the norms and social relations embedded in social structures that enable people to coordinate action to achieve desired goals." Harvard political scientist Robert Putnam describes it as "features of social organizations such as networks, norms and social trust that facilitate coordination and cooperation for mutual benefit."[19]

More recently Don Cohen and Larry Prusak, co-authors of *In Good Company: How Social Capital Makes Organizations Work,* suggest that social capital is a useful perspective for understanding behaviors that support or impede knowledge creation and sharing. In their view, "social capital consists of the stock of active connections among people: the trust, mutual understanding, and shared values and behaviors that bind the members of human networks and communities and make cooperative action possible."[20]

Some have suggested that people using the term are just pinning a new label on organizational culture, but social capital is only one feature of organizational culture. Culture consists of many different aspects, from artifacts to underlying belief systems. Prusak and Cohen are focusing on those qualities that indicate whether there is an environment of trust and connection demonstrated by cooperative action. So they are theorizing that there are specific conditions and behaviors that demonstrate high social capital.

What makes the focus on social capital particularly interesting right now is that it is one more example of the convergence in our understanding about business and other types of organizations. With social capital we find ourselves applying tools and terms, developed to understand society at large, to the dynamics within organizations.

So where would social capital fit within the framework shown in Figure 10.2? In my view, social capital is an expression of corporate identity and values in the center of the diagram. The purpose and values of an organization largely shape the culture, whether strong or weak, in characteristics such as social capital. Social capital is the organizational lubricant that supports knowledge sharing, collaborative work, and group decision making in every arena of value. It becomes particularly relevant in the expanded view of value that is suggested here. The social capital perspective is also valuable for considering the quality of relationships between participants and within communities that are part of the extended enterprise as well as those within it.

INTANGIBLES AND VALUE CREATION

Viewing intangibles as though they were assets moves us toward taking a whole-system approach to value creation. But it is only one step. In order to fully appreciate the power of intangibles, there are two additional, important perspectives to master—intangibles as negotiable goods, and intangibles as deliverables. We will consider these two qualities in Chapter 11.

CHAPTER ENDNOTES

[1] Thomas A Stewart, *The Wealth of Knowledge: Intellectual Capital and the Twenty-First Century Organization,* Currency Doubleday, 2001.

[2] Thomas A Stewart, *The Wealth of Knowledge: Intellectual Capital and the Twenty-First Century Organization.*

[3] Author Unknown, "Treasures Revealed," *CFO Magazine,* April 2001.

[4] Margaret M. Blair and Steven M. H. Wallman, *Unseen Wealth: Report of the Brookings Task Force on Intangibles,* Brookings Institute Press, 2001.

[5] Andrew Osterland, "Decoding Intangibles," *CFO Magazine*, April 2001.

[6] Karl-Erik Sveiby, *The New Organizational Wealth: Managing & Measuring Knowledge-Based Assets* (San Francisco: Berrett-Koehler, 1997).

[7] Margaret M Blair and Steven M.H. Wallman, *Unseen Wealth: Report of the Brookings Task Force on Intangibles*, Brookings Institution Press, 2001.

[8] Karl-Erik Sveiby, *The New Organizational Wealth: Managing & Measuring Knowledge-Based Assets* (San Francisco: Berrett-Koehler, 1997).

[9] Leif Edvinsson and Michael Malone, *Intellectual Capital: Realizing Your Company's True Value by Finding its Hidden Brainpower* (New York: Harper Business, 1997).

[10] Verna Allee, "The Value Evolution: Addressing Larger Implications of an Intellectual Capital and Intangibles Perspective, *Journal of Intellectual Capital*, MCB University Press, vol. 1, no. 1, 2000.

[11] Robert S. Kaplan and David P. Norton, *The Balanced Scorecard*, Harvard Business School Press, 1996.

[12] Robert S. Kaplan and David P. Norton, *The Balanced Scorecard*.

[13] Robert S. Kaplan and David P. Norton, *The Strategy-Focused Organizations: How Balanced Scorecard Companies Thrive in the New Business Environment*, Harvard Business School Press, 2001.

[14] Hazel Henderson, *Building a Win-Win World: Life Beyond Global Economic Warfare*, Berrett-Koehler, 1996.

[15] Deloitte and Touche Tohmatsu, *Corporate Environmental Report Score Card*, Deloitte & Touche, 1997.

[16] Tachi Kuichi and Bill Shireman, *What We Learned in the Rainforest: Business Lessons From Nature*, Berrett-Koehler, 2002.

[17] Shell Oil, *People, Planet & Profits: The Shell Report*, Summary 2001. Available through www.shell.com.

[18] Verna Allee, "The Art and Practice of Being a Revolutionary," *Journal of Knowledge Management*, MCB University Press, vol. 3,no. 2, 1999.

[19] Don Cohen and Laurence Prusak, *In Good Company: How Social Capital Makes Organizations Work*, Harvard Business School Press, 2001.

[20] Don Cohen and Laurence Prusak, *In Good Company: How Social Capital Makes Organizations Work*.

The great hope and opportunity offered by the intangibles perspective is that at long last we may be able to reconcile our business and economic models with the fabric of society and the web of life.

ELEVEN
Intangibles Go to Market

Intangibles are at the heart of all human activity, especially socioeconomic activity. However, understanding intangibles as assets, as in Chapter 10, is just the beginning. If we really want to understand the value dynamics of intangibles, there are two other very important dimensions to grasp. The first is how intangibles go to market—how they work as *negotiables* in economic exchanges. The second dimension is how intangible transactions take place—how they can be considered *deliverables*.

Intangibles, knowledge and benefits being among the most important, are the very foundation of value creation. We exchange or "trade" intangibles all the time as a key part of the way we do business. We can, of course, exchange knowledge for money in the form of a product or service. We also exchange knowledge for other knowledge when we socialize with our peers, participate in professional symposiums, or exchange expertise. Yet all this offering, trading, swapping, and exchanging of knowledge and other intangibles simply doesn't fit what is generally understand about how markets work. Or does it?

EXCHANGES

If we go back to the basics of economics we find the molecular unit of economic activity is the exchange. An exchange implies reciprocity, meaning the quality of the exchange is that it is fair or of comparable value. When something is extended from one person to another, there are two basic types of voluntary transfer. One is the *gift exchange*, and the other is an *economic exchange*. In the category of economic exchanges we find two major types: *barter exchanges* and *currency-based market exchanges*.

Gift Exchanges

A personal gift may be freely given with no thought or expectation of anything coming back. Anonymous donations fall into this category. The only reward is a feeling experienced in the giver that resonates with the anticipated happy and grateful feeling of the recipient.

Gift giving can serve as a way of deepening social ties within a community. In fact, it is essential for community. Anthropologists have found that communities do not need proximity, common language, religion, culture, or blood ties. None of these automatically leads to community, although they can be important secondary factors. The one activity communities have in common is reciprocity in gift exchanges.

Many social customs are actually rules about gift exchanges. What is an appropriate hostess gift when you are going to dinner at someone's home? The dinner of course is technically given freely, but there is an implicit social expectation that the recipient will return some token that expresses "thank you," or extend a similar invitation in return. In some cultures, a note or phone call a day or two afterward to express appreciation is all that is required. In other cultures, to show up at dinner without a reciprocal gift such as flowers would be a breech of social etiquette. So there is an implied "exchange" that is expected.

Barter Exchanges

Barter is another form of reciprocal exchange. A barter exchange is basically a one-time, negotiated deal. A barter trade happens between two parties who each have something the other wants. In localized economies barter can work pretty well. For convenience, people might negotiate their deals in a marketplace, which is simply a place where

Gift Economies

Gift economies have been around for thousands of years. San hunter-gatherers in Kenya maintain social networks by exchanging ostrich-egg shell beads, a tradition dates back 40,000 years and is still in practice. In 1950s a couple living with Bushmen in South Africa gave each women in the band a bracelet of cowrie shells as a parting gift. When they returned a year later, none of the shells were in the original group. They turned up at the edges of the region, in ones and twos in other people's ornaments. Through gift giving, the bracelets had spread across the community.[1]

We tend to think of gift societies as primitive. However, gift rituals can be extraordinarily complex and sophisticated. In the Pacific Northwest region of North America, the potlatch is a gift-giving event or party where gifts are given to the entire community. The gifts are to ensure future favors and gifts from the community, even from those who are not the immediate recipients of the gift. The quality and quantity of the gifts confer status and might even bring an honorific title such as "Whose Property was Eaten in Feasts."

people make exchanges. Marketplaces have been around as long as human society.

Economists generally tend to dismiss barter economies as primitive systems that exist only in a few pockets of culturally unique populations. They may be of interest to anthropologists, but barter and non-monetary exchanges are not at all considered relevant to the market economy. Barter is "messy," exceedingly complex, and very subjective.

However, if we look at business activity, we find there is an extensive barter system, involving intangibles, that plays a vital role in building both business relationships and the core dynamics of value creation. We are embedded in a complex and sophisticated barter economy that is deeply intertwined with the so-called market or monetary-based economy. This barter economy has been invisible to us, not because it doesn't exist, but because we have simply not bothered to notice how it operates in business. Our peripheral efforts to understand it have mostly involved social network analysis, looking at social ties and interactions. With the new focus on intangibles, perhaps we will find some new perspectives that will help us understand this complex barter system in economic terms.

Since barter is so messy, it is thought to be much simpler and more convenient to focus on financial transactions, which are assumed to be much more rational. To successfully barter, both parties have to have something the other one wants. If I want your camel but you don't want anything I have to offer, I can't make a deal with you. However, if we are members of a community with an agreed unit of exchange, say gold pieces, we can make a deal. I can trade my gold pieces (or a promise to pay you those gold pieces before some future date) for your camel. You, in turn can trade those gold pieces for something else that you want (or pay off a debt).

Currency-Based Market Exchanges

For a market to exist there must be a common, agreed unit of exchange, such as money. A marketplace is not at all the same thing as a market. For something to go to market, its value must be converted into agreed units of value. However, those units can be literally whatever people say they are: gold, pearls, beads, rice, pigs, chickens, tulip bulbs, horses, camels, flyer miles, dollars, yen, Euro. It doesn't really matter what the unit is, as long as everyone agrees to it. Then when someone wants to trade something, they simply convert the value of their good to the common unit of exchange and it can be available to anyone, without having to make a special deal every time it transfers hands.

Scrip also represents agreed units of exchange. In the 1950s, grocery stores issued trading stamps that could be redeemed later for other goods. A commonly-used scrip today is frequent flyer miles.

The market economy was ushered in when currencies and money became units of value. The market economy is the single most important—and powerful—element defining the industrial society because it allows goods to easily move from one's immediate local market to other marketplaces. Money, or currency, can be exchanged in the marketplace for anything. This allows people to use the agreed medium of exchange to obtain goods when they would not otherwise be able to cut a deal.

As a symbolic system, however, money is based on a whole set of assumptions, beliefs and social negotiations. Some work quite favorably overall and others can be problematic.

Money

Money has a huge impact on society and culture because money depersonalizes the exchange. That can be liberating, but it also destroys the context—the story of how a product came into existence. It becomes irrelevant where and how something was made, as long as it turns up in the market. Since the manner of production is irrelevant, it unfortunately also becomes invisible. We often no longer see the person making the shoes, building the cabinet, or stitching a garment, so we are less personally involved with the people who make most things we buy. One of the consequences of this is that any exploitation of people and resources that are part of production are quite often invisible to consumers. At an essential level, members of society have become disconnected from each other individually and as communities. If people had to walk through sweatshops filled with children, or through a stripped forest, they might feel differently about the products they purchase. But having money means we don't have to deal with those issues personally.

Not only is the product or material good depersonalized, so is the money. It doesn't matter where the flyer miles or the coin in your pocket came from or who "owned" them yesterday. Only the immediate question of ownership is important, and the history of the currency is unimportant. Its history ought to matter very much, because whoever has the right to issue the currency in the first place holds enormous power.

Money is not issued by governments, despite the fact that the U.S. Treasury might print the bills. Currency is actually issued by banks. Money can only move into circulation if someone goes into debt to the bank. To pay the debt off, more debt must be created. If you think this sounds suspicious, you are not alone. A growing number of people think this is a very unhealthy state of affairs. It not only makes economic growth dependent on debt; it concentrates power in the hands of those who issue the money—the banks.

To counteract these two serious drawbacks, and others, of the current monetary system, quite a number of communities are turning to more localized or community-based "complementary" currencies. Such currencies are units of measure that are agreed upon by the community of users. They can be social service hours or tokens of some kind, but they must be agreed to by a community for the currency to be viable.

How Do Intangibles Go to Market?

In every market there is a common, agreed unit of exchange. Even barter clubs use "trade dollars" to facilitate the exchanges. So the two traditional ways we have understood a trade or exchange are:

1. It occurs as a result of a personal, unique nonmonetary negotiation or barter, or

2. It is a depersonalized, indiscriminate offering and purchase in "the market."

With knowledge and other intangibles, there is no common unit of exchange. An executive team's knowledge about the competitive environment cannot easily be converted to a monetary value. Neither can your business network. But if one cannot assign a valuation to something, it cannot be traded in "the market," where money is the agreed unit of value.

This is not news to the intangibles crowd. Quite a number of them even consider this to be "the problem." These are the people trying to assign a value to intangibles so they can be traded in the market. Or they are trying to assess intangible value in monetary terms to place a value on the company. But to make such an attempt is to completely miss the point. It is simply the wrong question. This comes from believing that the old rules can be stretched just a little to include intangibles.

If *in*tangibles worked the same way as tangibles, they would not be called intangibles! So we need to stop trying to drag them back into our old models of value creation. They are *in*tangible and we must try to understand their market dynamics *as intangibles*, not by treating them like something else or trying to find a way to count them, like monetary units.

Intangibles actually go to market in two ways. They can be converted to monetary value and exchanged in the currency-based market. Or they can be bartered directly as intangibles.

Converting Intangibles into Monetary Value

Intangibles are offered for trade in the currency-based market when they have been packaged as a good or a contract with specific deliverables. When that happens, the intangible has been *converted* to another form of value. For example, someone could take his or her professional expertise and write a book. In this case, the intangibles of knowledge and experience have been converted to a *tangible* product that can be assigned value and can be offered or contracted for. Therefore, a knowledge product such as an industry report or an e-learning module that is sold for money must be considered as a *tangible*. These can be assigned a monetary value, can be traded in the marketplace, and can be accumulated as inventory.

Another, less attractive example of converting an intangible to monetary value, is the prevalence of companies making heavy financial contributions to political campaigns to curry political favors. The intangible being offered is political support on certain bills and measures in exchange for receiving a monetary campaign contribution. Of course, the practice of financial contributions to politicians in exchange for political favors is not confined to the United States.

Bartering Intangible Value

Intangibles also are put into economic play *without* being converted to a monetary value. When money is not involved in a trade, the trade is a form of barter. For example, one person may extend technical expertise to an associate in exchange for advice about marketing products. A deal has been made; knowledge has just gone to market. However, since no money has changed hands, the economic transaction is a barter exchange of intangibles—in this case, knowledge.

So intangibles are *negotiable*, meaning they can be exchanged for something else. They are a type of product or good that can be traded in the same way you would barter commodities. However, they don't actually behave the same way as tangible commodities.

The Multiplier Effect

With a tangible product or good, you must surrender possession when you trade it to someone else. With an intangible, however, you can trade it *and you still retain possession*, meaning you can extend the same intangible to someone else. In fact, when you engage in an economic knowledge exchange, both parties not only gain the other person's knowledge but they can actually create more knowledge of value to both of them. So the resource is not used up or diminished, and it can actually increase. One intangible that might be an exception to this is actual intellectual property, which can be sold to another outright. Also, the value of some knowledge does diminish when it is widely dispersed.

INTANGIBLES ARE DELIVERABLES

Since they can be bartered, given, or exchanged, intangibles are also *deliverables*. *Tangible* deliverables include anything that is contractual or expected by the recipient. If it is not delivered, then the contract, either explicit or implied, is not fulfilled. From that perspective, tangibles include any activity or transaction that supports the delivery of a product or service directly generating revenue.

Intangible deliverables involve knowledge and benefits that make things work smoothly and help build relationships. These are all those "little extras" that are not part of the contract and no one pays for directly. People will pay a premium for the intangibles associated with a service or product, but there is no explicit agreement that specific intangible knowledge or benefits will be included, nor can the tangible be quantified.

THREE ATTRIBUTES OF INTANGIBLES

So we see that in addition to being assets, as discussed in Chapter 10, intangibles are negotiable and are deliverables. The attributes of intangibles are discussed in greater detail in Table 11.1.

When we carefully consider these attributes, it becomes quite clear that intangibles are "real." Now, let's explore a method for making visible the usually unseen and unappreciated intangible contributions to value creation. We will start by unpacking the bundle of value in a typical business activity.

AN EXAMPLE OF HOW THIS WORKS

The molecular element in value creation is the exchange. Every exchange of value is supported by some *mechanism* or medium that

TABLE 11.1 *Three Important Attributes of Intangibles*

Intangibles are assets.

In the new thinking emerging from intellectual capital and triple–bottom line accounting, we have come to view intangibles as if they are *assets* that we can manage and measure, using nonfinancial scorecards. Intangibles, like other assets, are increased and leveraged through deliberate actions. Since knowledge management practices help build intangible assets, many people leading knowledge initiatives are also actively engaged in developing intangibles metrics and scorecards to build the business case for knowledge management.

Intangibles are negotiable goods.

Intangibles are negotiable economic offerings. We exchange intangibles all the time as part of the way we do business. We can, of course, exchange knowledge for money in the form of a product or service; that would be converting the intangible to a tangible. We also exchange knowledge for other knowledge. For example, one person might provide knowledge of how to animate PowerPoint slides in exchange for coaching on making a video. We also trade intangible benefits or favors. Perhaps an executive will grant someone access to their business or social network in return for their political influence on a regulatory issue.

Intangibles are deliverables.

Tangible deliverables include anything that is contractual or expected by the recipient, as part of the delivery of a product or service that directly generates revenue. Intangibles are all those large and small, unpaid or noncontractual, activities that make things work smoothly and help build relationships. *Intangible* deliverables include knowledge and benefits that can be extended from one person or group of people to another.

enables the transaction to happen. For example, if you and I want to exchange messages about a meeting, we may use the mechanism of e-mail or voice mail to support the exchange. One could make a house payment using either the mechanism of a written check or the mechanism of an online banking service. Any value exchange is supported by some mechanism that enables it to happen.

Figure 11.1 demonstrates both tangible and intangible exchanges. In this case, a technology provider would like to provide an online user

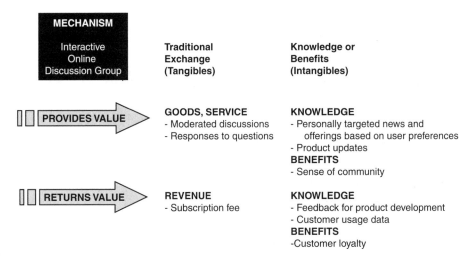

FIGURE 11.1 *Examples of value exchanges.*

group for its customers, for a small monthly fee. The mechanism is that of an online discussion group. This enables the creation of an interactive user group and supports several exchanges of value. The figure lists the value exchanges that might be enabled through such a mechanism.

In Figure 11.1, the traditional tangible exchange is the provision of moderated discussions, information, and personal responses to questions in exchange for a fee.

The intangibles of knowledge or information flow may involve gaining customer usage data and feedback for product development. As a result of their participation, the users receive the value-added exchange of personally targeted news or offerings.

By tracing the intangible benefits that accrue, one finds that the underlying logic for creating such a discussion group is not so much about gaining revenue from the service (indeed it may barely break even). The real goal for providing a user group may be to provide a sense of community on the part of the user. In return of course, one would hope to receive an increase in customer loyalty, which should result in increasing revenue. In this case, intangible value exchanges provide the real business logic for engaging in the activity.[2]

MAPPING THE VALUE EXCHANGE

Value *exchanges* can be described by means of a very simple mapping technique. With this foundation, it becomes possible to map virtually any enterprise or business network as a unique living system. Remember, living systems have physical exchanges and interactions, and they also have a cognitive aspect, that of an autopoietic network. Modeling exchanges of intangibles such as knowledge, that are key to a successful network, can help illuminate some of the significant cognitive pathways and interfaces from which new knowledge and innovation may emerge.

First we will define the terms "tangible" and "intangible" for the purpose of this method. The usage of these terms here may vary from the way others use them.

Tangible Goods, Services, and Revenue

Tangible exchanges involve goods, services, or revenue, including all transactions involving, but not limited to, contracts and invoices, return receipts of orders, requests for proposals, confirmations, or payments. Knowledge products or services that generate revenue, or that are expected and paid for as part of a service (such as reports or package inserts), are defined as a tangible and are depicted in the mapping as goods, services, and revenue.

Intangible Knowledge and Benefits

Intangible knowledge and information exchanges flow around and support the core product and service value chain, but are not contractually paid for. These include strategic information, planning knowledge, process knowledge, technical know-how, collaborative design work, joint planning activities, and policy development.

Intangible benefits are advantages or favors that can be extended from one person or group to another. For example, a research organization might ask someone to volunteer time and expertise on a project in exchange for an intangible benefit of prestige by affiliation. People can and do "trade favors" in order to build relationships.

The Map

Using the same example of the technology provider, we can "map" these value exchanges as a flow diagram showing both tangible and intangible exchanges; the mapping is shown in Figure 11.2.

The Service Provider provides technology support in exchange for a fee. Personalized offerings are extended to the customer to elicit feedback and usage data. That is an exchange of knowledge intangibles. What the technology provider is really trying to do is gain customer loyalty—again, an intangible exchange—this time an exchange of benefits.

The Three Elements of the Model

The diagram shown in Figure 11.2 employs the simple but versatile *HoloMapping*® technique. Ovals represent the Participants or roles. Participants send or extend Deliverables to other Participants. Arrows represent the direction the Deliverables are moving during a specific Transaction (see Figure 11.3).

Now, let's look at each of these elements in turn.

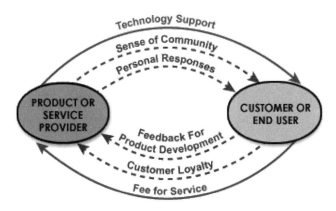

FIGURE 11.2   *Mapping the value exchanges.*

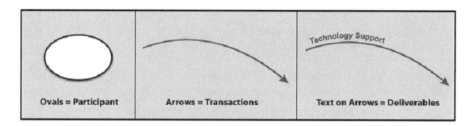

FIGURE 11.3   *Three elements of a HoloMap™ diagram.*

Participant

Participants are real people who are carrying out roles in the system. They are people or groups of people that have the power to initiate action, engage in interactions, add value, and make decisions. Participants can be individuals, small groups or teams, business units, whole organizations, collectives such as business webs or industry groups, communities, or nation states.

A Participant cannot be a database, a software program, or other technology. Humans may create technologies that mechanize certain tasks or fill a particular role (e.g., "reservations agent") but machines do not make their own decisions about which activities they engage in. Only people make those decisions, determining which activities and Transactions are important. People assign the tasks either to real people or to technology enablers that can complete the tasks.

In this mapping technique, we first focus on Participants and exchanges, then later consider what might be the most effective mechanisms to support completion of individual or group tasks. Participants or roles are represented by ovals or circles.

Transaction

Transactions or activities are represented by arrows. Each transaction originates with one Participant and ends with another. The arrow represents movement and denotes the direction of the transaction. In comparison to Participants or roles, which tend to be stable over time,

Transactions are temporary and transitory in nature. Transactions have a start, middle, and completion.

Arrows must be one-directional for the purposes of this method. An arrow depicts a single Transaction. Two-headed arrows are meaningless from the standpoint of actually managing anything or conducting a useful analysis. A double-headed arrow only shows that there is some kind of relationship. It does not tell us what the specific activity is, who is generating it, or where it actually ends.

Deliverable

Deliverables are the actual "things" that move from one Participant to another. A Deliverable can be physical or tangible, like a document or a table. Or, a Deliverable can be nonphysical, such as a message or request that may be delivered only verbally. It can also be an intangible Deliverable of knowledge about something, or a favor. It is the "what" that is most important, not the form that it takes. As communication and Internet technologies reduce our dependency on paper and "hard copy," the physical forms become less important. Here again, it is important to think of technologies as enablers of different activities and to focus on the Deliverables that are moving between Participants.

Exchanges in a Network

An exchange occurs when a Transaction results in a Deliverable coming back. The example given in Figure 11.4 suggests that there is always a reciprocal Transaction. This may or may not be the case in a real network.

An exchange may be delayed as several Transactions flow through different Participants, as in Figure 11.4. The diagram depicts the key exchanges in a network that consists of a manufacturer, distributors, assemblers, end users, and competitors. Find the arrow labeled "product information," that originates with the manufacturer. If you follow the thread of that intangible, you find that product information goes

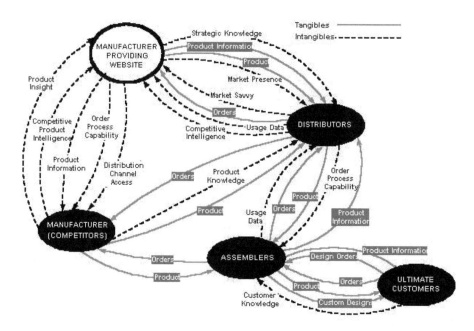

FIGURE 11.4　*A HoloMap diagram of exchanges in a network.*

from the manufacturer to the distributor, to the assembler, to the end user before generating the "return" of an order, which eventually comes back to the manufacturer.

Focusing on the exchange as the molecular element of value creation makes it possible to depict an infinite number and variety of value networks. An exchange depicted this way is a simplexity, a simple pattern and principle that can encompass enormous complexity. The exchange network is the basic *pattern of organization*. In Figure 11.4, we have defined a particular *structure* that is a manufacturing and distribution value network. The tangible exchanges depict exchanges of matter and energy (money), while the intangible exchanges depict cognitive and emotive exchanges such as favors and benefits.

In Chapter 12 we will go deeper into the mapping method. Then we will explore some of the particular nuances and benefits of the value network perspective.

CHAPTER ENDNOTES

[1] Bernard Lietaer, *The Future of Money: Creating New Wealth, Work and a Wiser World* (London: Century, 2001).

[2] Verna Allee, "Reconfiguring the Value Network," *Journal of Business Strategy*, July–August 2000.

© *2002 Hemera Technologies Inc.*

The molecular level of economic activity is the exchange.

TWELVE
The Value Network Perspective

Most of us spend a significant part of our day participating in at least one organization. Every organization has a unique pattern of interactions. These often seem at cross-purposes or counterproductive. Different parts of the organization can work against each other, suboptimizing the function of the whole.

Organizations are complex systems, frequently frustrating and difficult to work with—and there are simply too many variables to map or to fully understand. So why do we bother with models and maps?

Knowledge advances through symbolic systems, including the abstractions of ideas or models about how the world works. For example, the development of mathematics as a symbolic system has allowed us to build pyramids and fly to the moon and back. The invention of written language allows communications to exist through time. As our vocabulary of words and symbols increases, so do the abstract ideas they communicate.

Using maps, models, and symbols as business tools is not an attempt to describe ultimate reality. The purpose is to facilitate the communication of complex ideas. Such tools support different conversations about organizational life, each serving a different purpose.

Working with the method described in these few chapters is not going to magically make complex things simple. Any map, no matter how detailed, is certainly not the same as the territory itself. However, it can serve as a powerful visual tool to spark and support a particular type of conversation, illuminating some fundamental dynamics. If people are trying to explore questions about how value is created, what intangibles are important, which roles are critical, how complex processes interact with each other, or how the business really works, then the technique can be very useful.

From Engineered to Living Systems

Most of the models and tools of the past are "engineering" types of tools. They were developed to break down a complex system into its component parts or processes. Then, each of these could be fine-tuned and "engineered" for maximum efficiency and output, with the lowest possible amount of inputs and "friction" in the process. However, it doesn't work to try to then paste all those processes back together as an engineered whole system.

The popular model of the value chain is also an engineering concept, derived from expanding the process view to the business as a whole. But modeling a business as a value chain does not help us analyze the myriad of value-creating activities that take place across the enterprise. Even at the level of business units, the process view is inadequate to help us understand the most complex relationships and interactions.

Another danger in organizing around business processes is a tendency to embed them in rigid bureaucracies, technology systems, and structures such as ERP and SAP systems. If, for some reason, the process needs to be transformed, it is very difficult to change because so much structure is wrapped around it. That might be a good thing if you believe those processes will not change dramatically within the next five years or so. However, I can think of very few companies and industries for which this is a reasonable expectation.

But the most important drawback of the engineered process approach is that it completely ignores the individual. The focus is on physical systems and processes, not on individual action. One can engineer processes and physical materials; one can't engineer people.

People Are the Focus

That focus is completely backwards from a living systems perspective. Processes aren't the active agents in organizations—people are! When engineering approaches focus on processes, the cognitive and emotive aspects of the organization never show up in the business model. Engineering approaches are blind to the organizational intelligence that is embodied in real, living, breathing people. Small wonder investments in people are regarded as an expense!

So the first priority in moving to a living systems perspective is to have individuals and groups show up, front and center, as the active agents in the system. Any individual or group, of course, cannot manage a complex system. However, if I as an individual understand the most essential dynamics and guiding principles for my decisions, I can intelligently manage my role in that system and my own inputs, activities, and outputs. Even in traditional organizations, this basic principle of self-organization applies. And it is essential to master how it operates as we move into a world of organizational networks.

Mapping the Living System

What else would need to be part of a living systems perspective? Recall if you will the criteria for a living system from Chapter 4. There must be:

- *A pattern of organization* that is the configuration of relationships among the system's components, which determines the system's essential characteristics.
- *A structure* that is the physical embodiment of that pattern of organization.
- *Processes* for the key activities involved in the continual embodiment of the system's pattern of organization.
- *A pattern of cognition or intelligence* that is consistent with that of an autopoietic network.
- *Openness* to the flow of energy and matter.

The pattern of organization for living systems, including social systems, is the *network*. So that is the essential pattern we need to work with.

In Chapter 11, we identified the core activity or process of an organization as the *exchange*. We demonstrated a way to map exchange activity by identifying specific *Transactions* in which something flows between *Participants* as a tangible or intangible *Deliverable*. Participants are real people who are the active agents of the system.

Now, if we can describe the tangible and intangible exchanges that happen between people in a system as they form a network pattern, that should serve as a fairly good description of the unique structure of any organization. Through the pattern of exchanges that description can also reveal how open or closed the system is. Such an approach can move us much closer to a living-systems perspective of the organization. There would still be other aspects of intelligence to consciously work with in the "inner world" of the system, as was addressed in Chapters 8 and 9. However, this mapping approach is a good beginning for describing the dynamics of the "outer world" behaviors and aspects.

The Value Network

A value network is any web of relationships that generates both tangible and intangible value through complex dynamic exchanges between two or more individuals, groups, or organizations. People in organizations and enterprise networks engage in many different types of business interactions other than just exchanges of goods, services, and revenue. They also exchange knowledge and other intangibles such as favors and benefits in order to build relationships and ensure that everything runs smoothly.

These knowledge and other intangible exchanges are not just activities that support the business model; they are part *of* the business model. This is a very important difference between this approach and traditional business analysis. Viewing an enterprise as a value network brings greater understanding of the "real" business model than does traditional value chain thinking.

Virtually any purposeful organization or group can be understood as a value network, whether private industry, government, or public sector. So this view can also help explain the dynamics of economic clusters and national economies. Further, the same principles that describe large-value systems also play out at the business unit level and right on down to the shop floor and support functions.

Lately, there has been a lot of interest in alliance networks and business webs. In many cases there has been more hyperbole than substance, but there are some notable exceptions, including Kevin Kelly, author of *New Rules for the New Economy*[1], and the analysts with Digital4Sight group, whose findings have been published in *Digital Capital: Harnessing the Power of Business Webs*.[2] But industry-level networks are only one type of value network.

Other modeling techniques address some aspects of a business, but generally do not show the actual workings of the business model itself. Social network analysis, which has been around for over thirty years and was addressed in Chapter 8, is being used to some degree to understand the human interactions within organizations, but it does not readily lend itself to modeling the business dynamics. System dynamics is an excellent analysis method for modeling specific flows and their feedback loops, but, again, it does not lend itself to revealing the entire business model. Flow charts are limited to single processes and are too linear to show whole-system patterns.

Despite the interest, we have seen little serious work in developing *simple* and easily accessible business modeling techniques that take into account the role of *knowledge* and other *intangible* value exchanges as the foundation for these emerging networked enterprises. The goal of this method is to put in the hands of managers a tool that is easy to use, which will move people toward systems thinking.

ENTERPRISE AS A VALUE NETWORK

As traditional organizational boundaries become more permeable, organizational hierarchies become flatter, and decision making becomes driven out toward the edges, value network principles and dynamics are far more useful than traditional management tools. Value network modeling is not just a strategy technique; it is a tool for people at any level of an organization.

Much of the chaos that results from organizational change efforts arises not from trying to do something new, but from careless disregard of the complex system or systems that will be changed or affected in the process. Organizations evolve along multiple dimensions. When organizations change, old patterns of relationships are dismantled and reassembled into new configurations. People can better see where to make needed adjustments in their own activities without wreaking havoc on the whole system if they more fully understand the essential exchanges and relationships that create value.

The whole-system view of the value network approach shows how key processes work together. It shows dynamics such as feedback, interdependencies, flows, and exchanges. Further, it reveals the important role of knowledge and other intangibles, thus helping to identify business drivers and value opportunities.

Assessing the health and vitality of a value network requires understanding the overall patterns of exchange and determining the effect of tangible and intangible inputs for each Participant. Costs and benefits of each value-generating activity also must be calculated in both tangible impact and intangible terms. A deep analysis can provide a way to link system activity to scorecards.

The following diagrams, and those in Chapter 13, utilize the *ValueNet Works*™ modeling approach, a variation of the *Holo-Mapping*® whole-system diagramming technique developed by the author.

An Example[3]

Our example is a fictitious pharmaceutical company, PharmCo. In this instance, the people in the Sales and Marketing group would like to improve their ability to use customer feedback in developing new products.

The first step in the modeling process is to consider all the groups, both internal and external, that play key roles in the activities of the Sales and Marketing group. In this case, the four key groups (Participants) inside the company are *Sales and Marketing, Research, Product Development,* and *Manufacturing.* Key Participants outside the company are *Patients,* health care *Providers* such as doctors, *Payers* such as insurance companies, and *Regulators.* We then arrange these Participants as "nodes" for the network diagram as shown in Figure 12.1.

Now we are ready to start modeling the network dynamics.

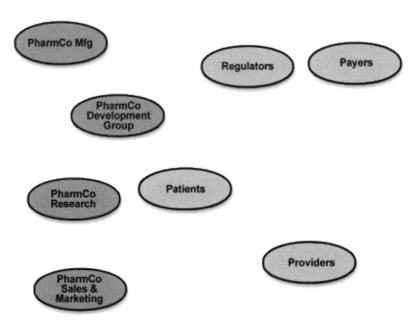

FIGURE 12.1 *PharmCo Value Network Participants. Here we show nodes that are internal to PharmCo in one color and those that are external in another.*

Mapping Tangible Transactions

First we will want to think about tangible exchanges that take place between the Participants. What are the core money-related Transactions? What are the tangible Deliverables in the system?

We can depict an activity, or Transaction, with an arrow originating from the group responsible or accountable for the Deliverable. The arrow shows the direction of movement and ends at the Participant who receives it or is affected by it. The label on the arrow names the Deliverable.

Figure 12.2 shows tangible Deliverables such as product candidates, process specifications, claims, payments, orders, and so on. In this case, the communication channel is considered a tangible Deliverable because it consists of data links, Web sites, and call centers that are paid for and hosted by PharmCo as part of the expected customer service support.

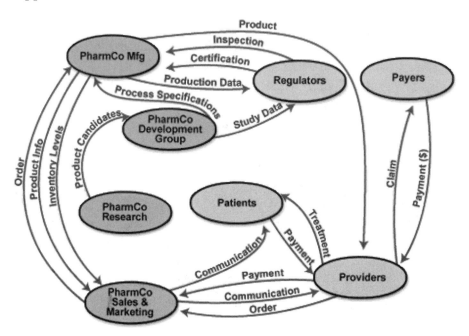

FIGURE 12.2 *Tangible Deliverables in the PharmCo Value Network.*

Mapping Intangible Transactions

We can depict an intangible transaction or exchange the same way. To help certain patterns show up more easily, use a different color or line style to distinguish the intangible Deliverables from the tangible Deliverables.

For PharmCo, one intangible is patient requirements. Another is disease knowledge, which PharmCo makes available through publications and its Web site. Others are informal assurances that Payers make to Providers advising that a new product will be covered, and reports to the Regulators of adverse reactions (see Figure 12.3). These are intangible because people do not pay for them directly, so they are not contractual or expected. They are extras, offerings extended to another Participant that help things work smoothly or that help build relationships.

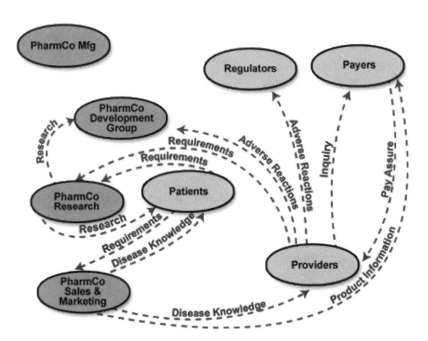

FIGURE 12.3   *Intangible Deliverables in a Value Network. The arrows are dotted to distinguish the transactions from the tangible transactions in Figure 12.2.*

Combined View

We now can pull together a whole-system view that shows how both tangibles and intangibles are working in the system (see Figure 12.4). When we diagram all these exchanges and Deliverables together, we have a picture of how the business really operates. Compared with more traditional modeling methods, this is a much truer picture.

The value network view of the enterprise helps us more fully understand the role of knowledge and other intangibles in value creation. The modeling process maps the most strategically critical intangible exchanges, allowing for easy targeting of value opportunities.

With this type of modeling technique and analysis, tangible and intangible scorecards can be linked directly to real business activities.

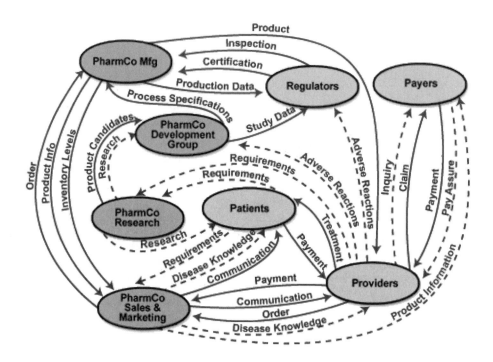

FIGURE 12.4   *PharmCo Value Network combined view.*

Whole-system views provide a visually compelling way to surface the logic and reasoning behind performance metrics. The contributions of intangibles to the business are specific and measurable. Even though monetary valuations rarely can be applied to intangibles, people can almost always come up with useful qualitative measures for them.

Patterns become visible with a whole-system perspective that simply can't be obtained with process mapping, no matter how sophisticated. I have used this method for a variety of projects, some of which are described in Chapter 13. Those projects address complex situations and interdependent processes ranging from product launch to environmental scanning for new technologies.

The Power of a Whole-System View—Example from Practice

One of my early projects was undertaken with a global technology company that was attempting to dramatically reconfigure its technical support system worldwide. My work with the firm was to provide support through its global benchmarking phase, in which the company would be sharing knowledge with several other companies outside its industry. The project would generate a huge amount of qualitative data, so I planned to develop a *HoloMap*™ with the group, to use as the foundation for a coded question set.

When I described the processes we would be going through, one of the team leaders insisted, "Oh, we don't need another map! We have been working with the quality tools for nine months and have completely mapped our process. We have made a number of improvements so there really isn't anything more to be gained from doing that."

"Well," I replied, "Flow charts and process diagrams often don't communicate well to another company because they are at a level of too much detail and are too company-specific. This will generate a whole-system view that will communicate more easily. Besides, it will only take us a couple of hours and we really need it to be able to handle the interview data." He reluctantly agreed to go along.

We assembled an international team at corporate headquarters and proceeded with the benchmarking preparation, including creating the system map. The process was going well, as I had made sure that all the key people representing the whole technology support system were in the room to participate. Then about halfway through the mapping, the room became silent. I quickly surveyed the room and saw that people were looking at each other strangely.

"What is it?" I asked, "What do you see?" Still silence! No one said anything. Finally, one of the team leaders stood up and walked over to the diagram.

"It's this," he said pointing to a particular Participant with quite a tangle of arrows going in and out. "If this group of people wasn't in the picture, everything would run so much smoother. You know," he added, "in nine months of working on this project, we never saw it."

I could tell from people's facial expressions that what he was suggesting would affect perhaps hundreds of people. "That sounds pretty serious," I ventured.

"It's very serious," he replied. "It's us!"

What I did not learn until later was that the company was planning a serious downsizing that would involve tens of thousands of people. This team was facing some very tough decisions and desperately needed to find a way they could provide effective technology support with considerably fewer people. This was exactly the breakthrough they needed to be able to reconfigure the whole technology support system. Much to their credit, they did it. They redesigned themselves right out of their jobs.

ANALYZING THE VALUE NETWORK

Analyzing the health and vitality of a value network requires addressing three basic questions. The first question, or analysis, is about assessing the dynamics of the whole system. The second and third questions concentrate on each specific Participant and that Participant's role in the value system. The basic analysis questions are:

- *Exchange Analysis*—What is the overall pattern of *exchanges* in the system?
- *Impact Analysis*—What *impact* does each value transaction have on the Participants involved?
- *Value Creation Analysis*—What is the best way to *create, extend, and leverage value*, either through adding value, extending value to other Participants, or converting one type of value to another?

I will address each of these questions in turn as we continue with our PharmCo example.

Exchange Analysis—Patterns of Exchange

Question: What is the overall pattern of exchanges in the system?

The story I just recounted represents the kinds of things people discover in an exchange analysis. Discoveries may not always be that dramatic, but invariably there will be insights and breakthroughs that could come only from a whole-system view.

One of the assumptions to start with is that every system works perfectly. It always fulfills its real purpose. Sometimes the real purpose can be quite different from the official purpose of the organization. Mapping the exchanges across the system often reveals the true purpose. For example, when I was working with a hospital group, the map showed quite clearly that the real customer of that particular health care system wasn't patients, or even doctors. It was the insurance companies that paid the claims. The entire system was set up to serve the needs of the payers at the expense of patients.

In the Exchange Analysis, we assess the overall patterns of value exchange to determine whether the value system appears healthy and sustainable and is expanding.

- Is there a coherent logic and flow to the way value moves through the system?

- Does the system have healthy exchanges of both tangibles and intangibles, or is one type of exchange more dominant? If so, why might that be?
- Is there an overall pattern of reciprocity? For example, is one of the participants extending several intangibles without receiving a fair return?
- Are there missing or "dead" links, weak and ineffective links, value "dead ends," or participant bottlenecks?
- Is the whole system being optimized, or are some Participants benefiting at the expense of others?

Sometimes a breakdown in value flow can be quite critical. Look for missing links, dead ends, or Participants that have become marginalized. Knowledge flow is especially critical for some companies. Let's look at the PharmCo example again.

In Figure 12.5, at least two patterns are noticeable. For one thing, the PharmCo Sales and Marketing group gains knowledge about requirements from patients, but that knowledge "dead ends" with them and is never passed on to PharmCo Research or to PharmCo Development. In fact, there is *no* significant knowledge exchange whatever between the PharmCo sales group and the research or development group. An Impact Analysis for Sales and Marketing would help address this situation.

Another pattern that shows up is that knowledge about a disease flows only one way. The Sales and Marketing group puts out information about certain diseases, but there is no channel for a two-way communication about disease with patients, providers, or payers. Even though PharmCo created a nice informational Web site to support a communication channel with patients and providers, it was being used only in a traditional marketing sense to broadcast information from the company about its products. Once this pattern became apparent, the company developed a new communication channel strategy that would create Web-based disease "communities." There the company's people could enter a real two-way knowledge exchange with their users and

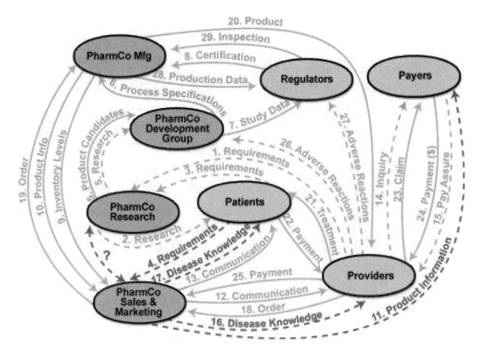

FIGURE 12.5   *PharmCo Value Network. The Exchange Analysis reveals missing links and dead ends.*

providers about important research, user feedback, and patient concerns.

Participants and Self-Organization

An individual or group cannot manage or change a whole system. However, people can and do self-organize to control their own activities. As network principles increasingly dominate the business landscape, it is vital that people taking action consider the health and vitality of the networks they are part of.

People must be skilled in analyzing both the value they are receiving from the system and the value they are contributing. Analyzing the impact of value inputs ensures that people and their organization are gaining positive value for every tangible or intangible input they receive.

Also, any Participant that is not contributing real value to the network as a whole will become increasingly isolated or may even be expelled. By the same token, any Participant that feels they are not receiving fair value for their participation is quite likely to withdraw. Carefully analyzing value outputs helps people find ways to increase both tangible and intangible value they can contribute to the system, thus strengthening their network ties and relationships.

The next two analysis steps provide this capability by looking at the specific inputs and outputs for an individual participant.

Impact Analysis—Value Transactions and Participants

Every input triggers some type of response. There are costs for handling the input and for leveraging the value received. Each input can directly or indirectly impact both the tangible and intangible asset picture. How is it helping increase the financial picture of the company? How is a particular input helping to build capability by increasing the competence of people, improving processes, or building better business and community relationships? These questions are addressed with an impact analysis.

An Impact Analysis answers the question, What are the tangible and intangible costs (or risks) and gains for each input for a particular participant? Using the model helps determine how each input:

- Generates a response or activity
- Increases or decreases tangible assets (cost/benefit)
- Increases or decreases intangible assets (cost/benefit)

Figure 12.6 shows the value inputs for the PharmCo Sales and Marketing group.

This view, combined with the initial whole-system Exchange Analysis, helped the Sales and Marketing group develop several new

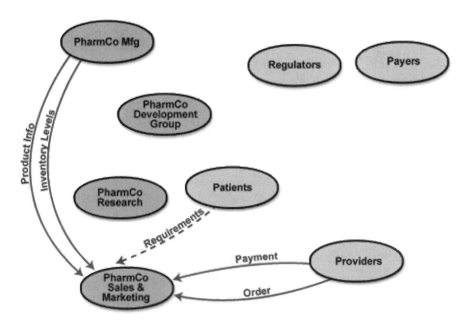

FIGURE 12.6   *Impact Analysis showing value inputs for PharmCo Sales and Marketing Group.*

ways of handling each input. The idea is to look at each of the inputs and explore the various costs and benefits it brings. Even though the view is from the perspective of a single Participant, there is consideration of the whole firm.

For example, the input of Requirements from Patients impacts the company in the following ways:

- It generates a follow-on activity of informal e-mails to pass along information.
- There are very small handling costs, so there is minimal negative financial or tangible impact. There is also no positive financial or tangible impact.
- There is a positive intangible impact because this increases the company's knowledge of the customer. However, the value gain is reduced because the knowledge does not get distributed

across PharmCo, but stops at Sales and Marketing. So the intangible benefit is also low.

Thus, the Impact Analysis for Requirements from Patients shows an overall cost/benefit ratio of low cost and low value.

After the Impact Analysis, the Sales and Marketing Group looked for ways to gain greater value from each input. For example, the group addressed the "broken link" between them and Research by more systematically handling customer input about requirements. Instead of using informal e-mail messages, they set up a simple routing and tracking system to be sure that customer comments were routed to Research and to other internal PharmCo Participants who could leverage the information. The routing change increased the benefit from low to high, with relatively little additional cost.

Value Creation Analysis

A Value Creation Analysis is similar to an Impact Analysis. This analysis focuses on one Participant at a time, analyzing how each Participant is extending value to other Participants in the system (see Figure 12.7).

What are the tangible and intangible costs (or risks) and gains for each value output for a particular Participant? Using the model helps determine how each value output:

- Adds new tangible or intangible value.
- Extends value to other Participants in the value network.
- Converts one type of value to another.

Each Participant can then assess each value output to determine:

- Activities, resources, and processes required.
- Cost/Benefit of each value-creating activity.

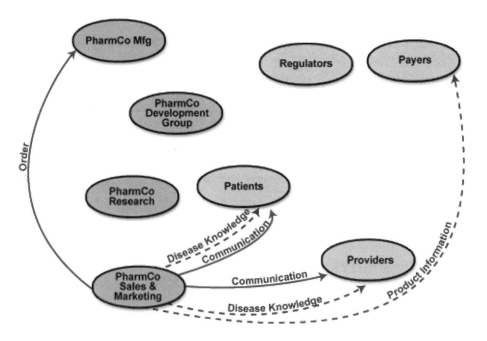

FIGURE 12.7 *Value Outputs for PharmCo Sales and Marketing Group.*

Value creation analysis can become very rich indeed. People usually see quite a number of ways they can increase their value outputs, especially by leveraging the intangible value they generate.

For a value network to be healthy and viable, overall positive value inputs and outputs must be greater than negative or neutral contributions. Therefore, a value creation analysis isn't really complete until the Participant also understands what impact a particular output has on the Participant who receives it.

A perfect example of this is the story of a financial services company that maximized efficiencies in its client reports. The company's overall cost benefit analysis was excellent from its viewpoint. However, a closer analysis showed that its efficiencies had greatly inconvenienced the customers. Customers had to spend so much time making the reports compatible with their own system that they actually saw receiving the report as a negative value input. Oops!

The clear message is that self-organizing does not mean selfish organizing. It means managing your own activities in a way that is good for you, good for the other participants, and good for the value network as a whole. Without a whole-system perspective and understanding, and employing whole-system principles, self-organization doesn't work.

WHAT MAKES THIS METHOD DIFFERENT?

Since this view includes core business processes, people sometimes ask if this isn't just another way to show business processes. But the typical process diagram indicates nothing about the whole-system context for that process—you can't see the whole system. With a whole-system view you can see all the key processes and how they are working together plus a whole lot more, from a nonlinear perspective that allows larger patterns to become visible.

This approach supports several very important shifts of perspective and lends itself to a variety of views and analysis techniques. For example, the diagramming process can be enriched by sequencing the Deliverables. This illuminates the processes in the system as a step-by-step story of the key activities. Arranging the sequenced activities into various types of tables allows in-depth analysis and creation of detailed corporate scorecards. One view might help a company reduce time for product launch; another might improve knowledge transfer of an important innovation. A value network analysis also can be combined and linked with other diagramming approaches to provide a multidimensional view of the enterprise.

The power of the method lies not in that it does any one of these, but in that it does *all* of them with one simple basic method. This approach:

- Moves the business perspective from an engineered process view to that of a dynamic living system in a way that maintains the basic integrity of the processes.

- Honors *people* as the active intelligent agents of value creation.
- Reveals important cognitive pathways for knowledge sharing.
- Includes emotive exchanges such as favors and other intangibles.
- Shows the boundaries of the system being scrutinized.
- Shows all the key Participants, even those engaged in nonfinancial Transactions.
- Shows all the key Deliverables along with the originator and recipient of each one.
- Shows the most critical tangible and intangible inputs and outputs for each Participant.
- Shows all the key Transactions.
- Sequences transactions to show time relationships.
- Can reveal important whole-system feedback loops.
- Allows the development of tangible and intangible performance metrics that are linked to specific business activities.
- Can be used for every level of a system, from work teams to economies.
- Creates diagrams that can nest with diagrams from other levels.
- Works equally well for government agencies, nonprofits, and nongovernmental organizations, as well as for private businesses.
- Can be used for an infinite variety of organizational systems, capturing their uniqueness instead of forcing them into an artificial model.

In Chapter 13, we will look at several different examples from actual practice that use the mapping method. Then we will move on to addressing some of the insights and ethical issues emerging as we move into a more networked world.

CHAPTER ENDNOTES

[1] Kevin Kelly, *New Rules for the New Economy*, Viking Press, 1998.

[2] Don Tapscott, David Ticoll, and Alex Lowy, *Digital Capital: Harnessing the Power of Business Webs*, Harvard Business School Press, 2001.

[3] Verna Allee, "Evolving Business Forms for the Knowledge Economy," *The Handbook of Knowledge Management*, Clyde W. Holsapple, ED. Springer-Verlag, 2002.

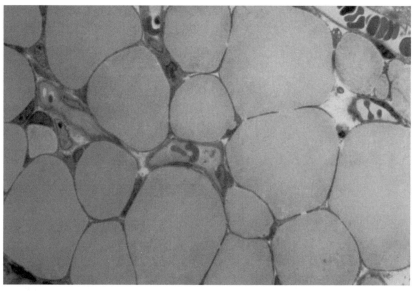

© *2002 Hemera Technologies Inc.*

The best models are as simple as possible,
But no simpler.

—Albert Einstein

THIRTEEN
Value Network Examples

Mapping organizations with rather messy looking "spaghetti and meatball" diagrams might feel unorganized to people who are more comfortable with tightly-engineered diagrams such as process schematics. In fact, such an exercise might feel like a step backward instead of a step forward.

But living systems *are* messy, especially if they are social systems involving real people. And real people need to personally find themselves in the system before they can begin to comprehend its workings or self-organize to support it. When mapping value networks, the goal is not to get to a perfect diagram. The diagrams are merely visual aids and "moment-in-time" snapshots. The goal is to be able to hold a conversation in which whole-system issues can be easily addressed. The method does not rely on some system "expert" or observer to validate the diagram. Validation comes through the participants themselves, who are describing their own lived experience in the organization. This simple, visual vocabulary helps people surface and talk about their mental models, which is an essential capability for organizational learning.

THE CHANGING GAME OF BUSINESS

If organizations are living systems, then it makes sense to think about different ways they might interact with the environment. Seeing a business as an ecosystem means thinking about its relationships differently and offers an opportunity to reframe the business or redefine its role. Many of the innovations in business models result from employing rules of engagement that are more organic than traditional bureauracies.

Let's return for a moment to the example used at the end of Chapter 11 (see Figure 11.3). That same diagram, shown in Figure 13.1, is a value network model of a clothing manufacturer, showing how knowledge and intangibles can be leveraged in an Internet strategy.

The manufacturer made a strategic move into e-commerce by providing free marketing Web sites to its distributors. In this case, the manufacturer also allows competing manufacturers to sell products via the same Web site. Why on earth would the company create a marketing channel for a competitor?

Selling competitors' products on the Web site makes sense only if we understand the flow of knowledge and intangible benefits that the manufacturer gains. This savvy company focuses on these flows of knowledge and intangibles to build closer relationships with its end

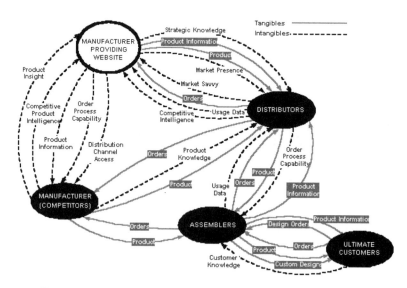

FIGURE 13.1　*Internet-enabled value network.*

users. In the process, it gains market intelligence, customer feedback, and competitive intelligence. The company shares knowledge of products and markets not only with the distributors but also directly with its competitors. Incidentally, this situation is also an excellent example of what Adam Brandenberger refers to as co-opetition.[1]

REWRITING THE RULES OF KNOWLEDGE SHARING

The full potential of value networks has been brought home by the overwhelming success of Cisco, the dominant company in Internet routers. Cisco completely changed the rules about knowledge sharing with partners and customers, garnering widespread attention for the phenomenal success of its business model.

In 1997, a team of researchers working at Digital4Sight in Toronto used this value network methodology to examine up-and-coming e-commerce companies.[2] Cisco was already gaining a reputation for being a good company to partner with. It was also noted for its use of Web technology to support a free exchange of information with customers.

But when the full pattern of knowledge and intangibles surfaced during the analysis, it readily became apparent just how good a partner Cisco was. Figure 13.2 shows the value network exchanges. Frequent exchanges of knowledge (e.g., sharing strategic knowledge with partners) dominated the business model. Mission-critical intangible exchanges outnumbered key tangible exchanges by two to one!

Note that the "real" business model includes competitors and standards groups, even OEMs, with whom the company never exchanges money or tangible goods. The configuration of competitors and standards bodies is especially important, because favorable standards are an important intangible benefit that can make or break a technology company. If this were a more traditional business model, these participants would never show up because they are not engaged in direct financial transactions.

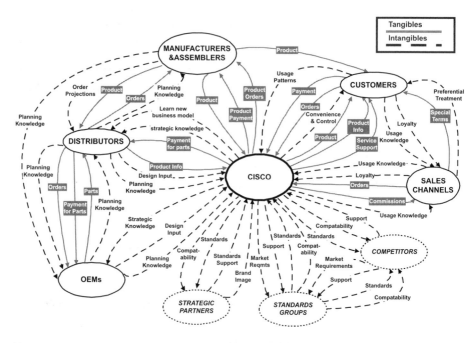

FIGURE 13.2 *Cisco Systems value map. (Courtesy Digital4Sight.)*

DEFINING COMPETITIVE ADVANTAGE

S.A. Armstrong Ltd. is one of the top companies it its field in North America. It is a Canadian engineering and manufacturing company providing heavy equipment that is used in commercial building construction. Company CEO Charles Armstrong led the company to become one of the early adopters of intellectual capital measures and knowledge management strategies. He has long been making the argument that intangibles are critical for every business, not just companies in high-tech or knowledge services, but his claims often fell on deaf ears in his very conservative industry and even within his own company.

We spent one morning creating a value network map of the company. Charles didn't say a word to anyone else in the company about what it was; he just taped the drawing up on a wall in the conference room and left it there. Over the course of the next three weeks, people would use the room. Being curious, they would look over the diagram. In ones and twos, they started asking Charles about it and spending a few minutes with him in conversation about it. Sometimes they would point out something he had missed, or challenge why a particular exchange was there, or why it was so important.

One thing that became quite apparent from the diagram (see Figure 13.3) is that the company provides a lot of intangibles in the form of knowledge sharing—running seminars, providing free software, and generally engaging in an open exchange with its primary customers.

Another important intangible for Armstrong is an explicit promise to support the customer and help minimize risk when unexpected situations pop up, as they often do on large-scale construction projects. That promise is backed up by action and is one of the reasons the company enjoys its reputation for excellent service.

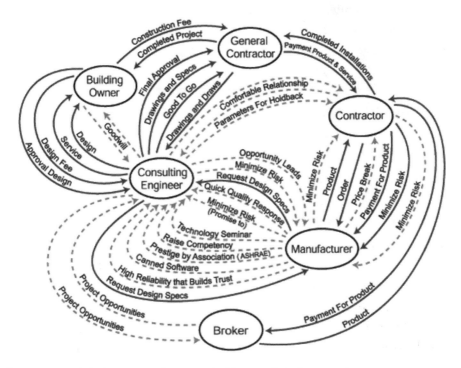

FIGURE 13.3   *S.A. Armstrong value network. (Courtesy S.A. Armstrong.)*

The conversations that people were having about the diagram began to work a subtle change in people's perception of the business. They began to realize that all these "extras" were the very things that gave them competitive advantage in their market. Other companies might provide similar products, but they could not match S.A. Armstrong in service. The intangibles are not only their market differentiator but are also extremely hard for other companies to imitate. Their intangible deliverables are so much a part of the company philosophy and culture that it would take a major effort for another company to create the same conditions.

Now when Armstrong engages with an important new customer or wants to improve an existing relationship, managers have a customer conversation using the mapping process. In one case, a new customer Armstrong was acquiring was a family-owned business that was changing leadership from father to son. When we mapped their value network, it provoked a surprising and positive emotional response. The map showed that although the company has less than 100 employees, over the years it had evolved into a value network that effectively manages hundreds of key relationships. The mapping process was a powerful way of validating the years of hard work, and assured the founder that his son understood the complex web of relationships that are key to the company's continuing success.

THE COMPANY OF ONE

In their best-selling book, *Enterprise One to One,* Don Peppers and Martha Rogers make the point that every customer is unique.[3] In the current economic environment, success comes from meeting each customer's distinctive needs. This is the main idea behind customer relationship management (CRM). The goal is to know your customers so well individually that you can make a particular and personal offering available, even if there is only one customer who needs that feature.

Why not begin to think in terms of the company of one? Every company is unique. No two companies, even in the same industry, are organized exactly the same way, with exactly the same number of people filling the same roles or managing the exact same processes and deliverables. The variation between companies is the difference that makes a difference. It is far more interesting to understand how companies are special and unique than how they are the same.

Every business model is unique and every configuration of a value network has its own pattern and identity. Intangible exchanges offer important clues to the guiding principles, agreements, and values the company holds. The network patterns also reveal disconnects between what a company says it values or provides and what it actually does.

Moving from Linear to Nonlinear Process Analysis

Volunteer associations are masters at creating value networks. Any purposeful organization requires a healthy exchange of tangibles and money to support its infrastructure and to ensure delivery of its core services. Not-for-profit organizations are particularly rich in intangible exchanges, because intangibles are often their primary deliverable to the community. Associations also weave richly textured social tapestries of volunteers, administrators, and affiliate associations.

The local branch of a health care services organization undertook a major assessment and evaluation of its volunteer helpline unit to try to improve services and speed response time. As part of the evaluation, consultants Lisa Faithorn and Kathy Cody conducted a mapping exercise during a group retreat. There was already an existing "official" process map of how the helpline was supposed to work (see Figure 13.4(a)).

The flow chart looked very neat and orderly on paper, but the experience of the helpline unit volunteers did not at all match the process flow chart! Over time, a number of informal side processes had evolved to maneuver around the linear constraints of the process model. As a result, it was taking too long for new volunteers to become familiar with the ways things really worked and to be effective.

The mapping exercise moved the focus away from the linear depiction of the process and oriented instead to real people who were fulfilling different roles. It quickly became apparent that simple items on the flowchart actually were quite complex, involving several different people and requiring continuing activities throughout the entire process (see Figure 13.4(b)).

Even though the new map looked a bit messy and busy, everyone agreed that it accurately depicted how the helpline really worked. It also showed all the intangible "extras" that people were responsible for that did not show up in the flow chart.

The goal was not to map the entire organization or system. The method was used to describe a complex, nonlinear process that previously had been artificially forced into the linear flow diagram.

Shifting to a nonlinear modeling technique revealed not one but *three* deeply enmeshed and interdependent processes that could have variable time relationships with each other. The group teased apart

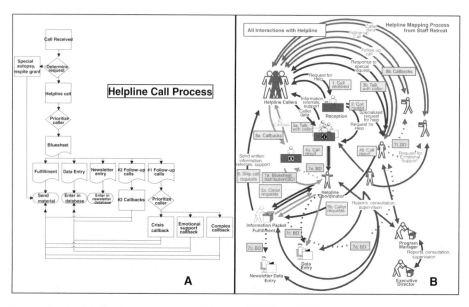

FIGURE 13.4   *(a) Existing process map of how the Helpline Call Process was supposed to work. (b) Nonlinear map of exchanges across the unit, showing how things really happened.*[4]

diagram 13.4(b) to create three new maps depicting the three core processes. (Figure 13.5)

In the process of developing the diagrams, the group also addressed and resolved numerous policy issues regarding the handling of calls. They clarified their recruiting criteria for volunteers and moved to a much deeper understanding of the role of the helpline as a component of the extended association services. With some refinement, the diagrams also became an orientation tool for new volunteers.

EXTENDING VALUE TO THE COMMUNITY

York Hospital in Maine noticed that the success of a patient's stay was linked to the level of support the patient had at home before, during, and after the hospital stay. The hospital staff was quite efficient at handling patients once inside the hospital, but that simply wasn't enough. To ensure patient success they created PATH (patient approach to health) teams, groups of people who built strong relationships with community service groups. The teams follow the patients through their entire "path" of care.

Figure 13.6 reveals the core tangible and intangible exchanges of York Hospital's PATH teams. In this model, the teams are organized geographically so the PATH team can more easily interact with social services groups in the local community.

Patient satisfaction and recovery rates have improved significantly with this model of health care. Yet, one can readily see that the PATH team has few tangible outputs or deliverables compared to the amount of intangible knowledge and benefits that they extend to others.[5]

The York Hospital example demonstrates how embracing a value network perspective begins to expand the value of the system to the larger community. It is helping to improve the prosperity of the community by making available a resource team to families that are experiencing a health-related absence of a family member. This team might arrange for child care, make sure that transportation needs are

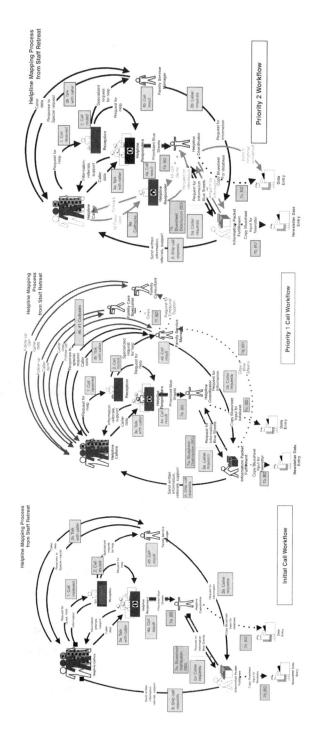

FIGURE 13.5   *Maps of three concurrent processes that gave people a much stronger sense both of the whole and of their own roles in the system.*

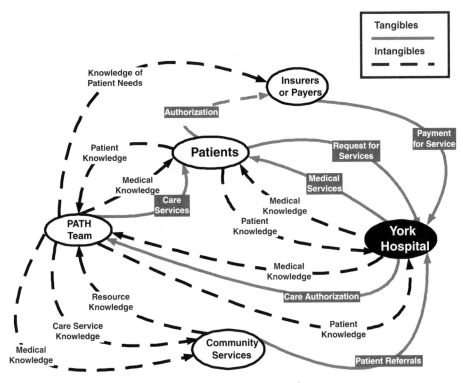

FIGURE 13.6   *York Hospital and PATH team business model.*[6]

covered, or work with social service organizations to provide in-home follow-up care medically and personally.

Any time services become affordable and available to people who formerly did not have access to them, overall prosperity increases. Intangible value is real value that brings social good to the recipient. Increasing intangible value offerings expands wealth, not only in personal terms but also in the overall sense for the community.

EXPANDING PROSPERITY

For the most part, people think that an organization or company must be focused either on providing social goods and intangibles or on making a profit. The two types of value have been generally thought of as a polarity. You can do one or the other, but you can't really do both. Yet one very successful company pioneered a business model that does generate both profits for the owners and prosperity for the participants.

eBay, the online auction site, has been featured in many articles in the business press. It is one of the few "dot-com boom" Internet businesses that continued to thrive during and after the e-commerce downturn in 2000. It has even shown a profit, earning $90.4 million on $9.3 billion in gross merchandise transactions in 2001.[7]

eBay operates with a principle of complete transparency and a clear intent for everyone in the eBay network to be successful. They charge a small initial listing fee and a small percentage of each winning bid. Therefore, there are no hidden costs and no escalation of the investment needed to offer items for sale.

Through a simple rating system and purchaser comments, everyone's experience with every other participant is also transparent. Unscrupulous sellers are quickly exposed, and people simply do not do business with them. eBay also has strong community elements in that people who do not hold to the community values aren't voted out, the community simply stops engaging in exchanges with them.

The company first came to my attention in 1997, when I was a member of the analysis team for the Digital4Sight study.[8] (For perspective, at that time, eBay's Web site was black and white, in courier typeface, and it went down often.) But we were intrigued with what was revealed in the pattern of exchanges when we mapped the business model. The balance of tangible to intangible exchange and the pattern of reciprocity unfolded like a beautiful flower (see Figure 13.7).

What makes eBay especially interesting is how it demonstrates the potential for a value network to expand prosperity. Because of eBay, quite a number of people who had not been able to earn income suddenly had a way to participate in the economy. Others found that a hobby could be leveraged to create additional income. As of early 2002, there are 30,000 to 35, 000 of eBay's sellers that make online trading their primary livelihood.

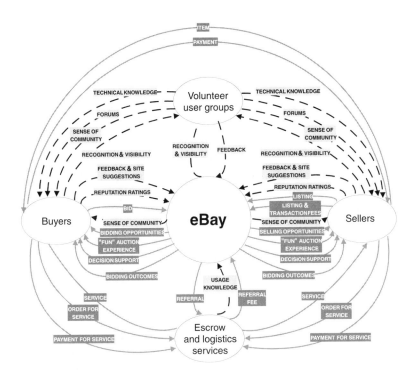

FIGURE 13.7   *eBay value network. (Courtesy Digital4Sight.)*

Another aspect of increasing prosperity is the way the company has provided a vehicle for recycling millions of consumer items. Although many items are collectibles, others are consumer items that people might have purchased new. Even though the company clearly benefits from the prevalent consumer culture, even a small degree of reduction in consumption of raw materials for new products can be seen as an overall good for society.

The paradox is that these types of sales are "invisible" economic transactions. MIT economist Lester Thurow says, "E-Bay sales will never show up in the GDP (gross domestic product) as a measure of the economy, but they do affect real income. Keep in mind that we have a set of losers here, the guys who used to make a living doing transaction costs." Thurow's category of losers includes professional dealers who collect "middle man" fees and newspaper classified ads.

Thurow notes that newspaper classified advertising has declined since eBay moved into handling used automobiles.[9]

INCREASING PROSPERITY THROUGH INTANGIBLES

We are beginning to see an interesting convergence in which businesses are becoming more like networked communities, and in some cases, networked communities are becoming more like businesses. An artist association that opens galleries or manages Internet marketplaces would be an example of a value network focused primarily on intangibles, yet finding ways to increase tangible transactions. Some of this is happening organically through natural evolution. In other cases, it is happening more deliberately, and Friendly Favors is an example.

Sergio Lub, a California jewelry designer and entrepreneur, launched his jewelry business by traveling the world and creating a web of people selling his jewelry. He has long had a keen interest in community economics and community exchanges in particular. On his travels to about seventy countries, including some with very hard economies and war zones, he discovered an important economic principle. "Happy people are those who are the most generous," he found. "The more one gives, the more other people give, and there are suddenly more apples in the tree to eat."

He gives the example of one woman who started collecting clothing to give to poor children in Central America. Others learned of what she was doing and began bringing her the clothing their children had outgrown. She now has a garage full of clothes, and the more she gives away the more she gets. It just keeps growing. Sergio grew curious about how certain communities and webs of friends, as in the example, can so easily create greater prosperity, while others do not.

At a State of the World Forum, Sergio heard speaker Steve Rockefeller comment that the overhead of the Rockefeller foundation was greater than the money the foundation gave. After Rockefeller's talk, the head of the largest NGO in Sri Lanka stood up in the audience and told him that for every two dollars they receive it costs them a dollar to pay consultants to fill out the forms for the Rockefeller Foundation.

Sergio thought about that statement and contrasted this with another organization he was familiar with, the MacArthur Foundation, which also gives away millions each year. He knew that institution was successful in allocating real financial help without such a cumbersome grant-based system. The MacArthur people look for those who are already doing good work or ask their circle of trusted friends for recommendations. Then, with minimal paperwork, they send a check.

In the State of the World forum discussion, it had come out that the challenge for the Rockefeller Foundation was the ability to trust that the cause was a worthy one. This was far less an issue with the MacArthur Foundation. Would it be possible, Sergio wondered, to extend that principle of referral by friends? Would it be possible to set up a system in which people can recommend good work, the referral system could not be manipulated, and people who are doing good things could find each other?

Out of that question, Friendly Favors was born. Friendly Favors (www.friendlyfavors.org) is an online community that was launched in August 1999. As of spring 2002, there are 11,442 members, living in 134 countries.

It is a completely voluntary association of people who acknowledge one another by awarding *Thankyous,* that are tracked on the Web site. Membership is free and open to all, but a new member must be sponsored by an existing member, thus building a chain of trust across the network. When someone logs on to the site as a member, they make an offering to the community of something they can provide to other members free or at a substantial discount. Members who take up the offers can give each other *Thankyous* for the favors they receive, which is deducted from their own pool of *Thankyous.*

The shared purpose of the community is to support people who are committed to building a sustainable world that works for all. A guiding principle is that members report generous acts and encourage more goodwill by sending *Thankyous*. The system serves as a complementary currency through which intangible favors are rewarded, creating intangible benefits of goodwill and reputation as well as economic benefit in the form of reduced cost for real services. *Thankyous* cannot be converted to money, but they can entitle people to discounts.

This remarkably simple premise has established a value network that increases prosperity through the deliberate use of intangibles. The fact that it works is not an accident. A number of people who are interested in monetary systems are members of the network and help the group make conscious decisions about the way it works. It is an example of the way people are engaging in direct bartering of intangibles, moving beyond the confines of the purely monetary transactions that were proving so burdensome to the Rockefeller Foundation. They are finding ways to deliberately leverage the intangible economy to increase prosperity and contribute to the greater good.

INFINITE VARIETY

The object in constructing any dynamic model is to find the unchanging laws or principles that generate the changing configurations. The whole-system approach to modeling business dynamics, based on the principle of exchange, allows us to explore not just a few organizational forms but thousands. It also serves as an indicator of the mental and managerial skills an organization will need to expand its capacity for true systems thinking and mastering the integrative mode of cognition and knowledge creation. As our knowledge increases, we can expect to see more methods emerging that truly support systemic thinking.

With a value network perspective, people can gain new insights into managing their own organizations more effectively. More important, they can also find pathways to generate greater value for their own benefit, for other members of their value network, and for the good of society and the planet. Indeed, the terms "for profit" and "not-for-profit" may become obsolete as people appreciate that every organization is a network of real people exchanging both tangible and intangible value.

CHAPTER ENDNOTES

[1] Adam M Brandenberger, Jerry L Nalebuff, and Ada Brandenberger, *Co-opetition: 1. A Revolutionary Mindset That Redefines Competition and Cooperation; 2. The Game Theory Strategy That's Changing the Game of Business,* Doubleday, 1997.

[2] Don Tapscott, David Ticoll, and Alex Lowy, *Digital Capital: Harnessing the Power of Business Webs,* Harvard Business School Press, 2000.

[3] Don Peppers and Martha Rogers, Ph.D., *Enterprise One to One: Tools for Competing in the Interactive Age,* Currency Doubleday, 1997.

[4] Lisa Faithorn and Kathleen Cody, "Helpline Core Service Evaluaton Final Report," O'Neil & Associates, 1999.

[5] Elizabeth Reuthe and Verna Allee, "Knowledge Management: Move the Case Model From a Snapshot to a Story," *Health Forum Journal,* May/June 1999.

[6] Elizabeth Reuthe and Verna Allee, "Knowledge Management: Move the Case Model from a Snapshot to a Story."

[7] Susan Brownmiller, "The eBay Obsession," *My Generation,* May/June 2002.

[8] Don Tapscott, David Ticoll, and Alex Lowy, *Digital Capital: Harnessing the Power of Business Webs.*

[9] Susan Brownmiller, "The eBay Obsession," *My Generation,* May/June, 2002.

© 2002 Hemera Technologies Inc.

Everything has both intended and unintended consequences. The intended consequences may or may not happen; the unintended consequences always do.

—Dee Hock

PART V

Principles for Prosperity

FOURTEEN
New Business Fundamentals

Not too far from my house is a high ridge that runs through one of the huge regional parks in the area. Even though cattle still graze the hills, much of the ecosystem remains intact. Golden eagles fly overhead, and walkers here may glimpse deer, coyote, fox, and even a mountain lion. Thick stands of oaks and chaparral in the shaded valleys yield to rolling grassland on the sunny high slopes. When I walk through this park, I am a universe of networks looking at other living networks nested in still more networks of forest and grasslands. All are held in the precious web of life that connects us all.

Networks are the natural pattern of organization in living systems. They are the pattern of social systems and the natural pattern of business relationships as well. Even our most critical technology for the knowledge economy, the Internet, is self-organizing according to network principles. Social networks act as organizational neural networks for us to collectively notice what is going on around us, to learn, think, and reason together and take intelligent action. Companies and organizations with network patterns are themselves nodes in larger business webs and economic clusters.

Wherever one system nests within another in this way, we find another characteristic of living systems, that of holarchy. Holonic organization means systems are embedded in other like systems. Our bodies are organized this way. Networks of DNA are embedded in networks of cells, which are embedded in networks of organs and circulatory systems, and so on as we progress to ever larger systems and ecosystems.

Human society reflects holonic organization. Individuals are embedded in families that are part of communities, which are part of national and international communities. Business also reflects holarchy as individuals and entrepreneurs serve or work for businesses that in turn serve other businesses, which participate in industry clusters that together comprise whole economies.

What appears to be different levels of systems—is *one system*, viewed from different vantage points. The world of business is a vast holonic web of organizations patterned as networks nested within other networks. The same essential pattern of organization plays out in infinite variations, forms, and structures, all organizing themselves according to the same pattern and principles.

THE CREATIVE EDGE

The great challenge of organizational life is how to have stability while being flexible enough to adapt and change. When complex systems of any kind (swarms of bees, businesses, economies) are at the edge of chaos, the place where there is neither too little structure nor too much, they produce complex adaptive behaviors. With too much structure they can't move; with too little they disintegrate or fly apart. Companies that have learned to keep that edge—that fine balance between tight and loose—are at their most alive, creative, and adaptable. But it is easy to slip from the edge into rigidity on the one side or into disintegration on the other.

To be sustainable, organizations must appropriately balance order and disorder and do this in a way that is compatible with the larger environment. Organizations follow the same principles of entropy as living systems. Entropy refers to the amount of free energy that is available versus "bound energy" that is locked up in some way and not available for use. Living systems balance the disorder of free energy with the order of bound energy.

It is important to understand that there is no one right answer for order, nor is there one right answer for how we structure our businesses. Trying to find one formula is a waste of effort. As patterns of roles, interactions, and relationships, *all* organizations are networks. Individual structures however, may be very different. The creative edge can be maintained with many different forms, according to what is happening in the environment.

For example, one structure may be a tightly constrained network with a rigid hierarchy of subdivided roles and tasks and a strong administrative apparatus. That structure, a bureaucracy, may be successful in a stable and slowly evolving environment, but it would be too rigid and bound to compete successfully in a more chaotic environment. In contrast, a more loosely connected company that is successful in a rapidly changing environment might not be successful in one that is more stable.

The ability to consciously work with the business model is proving to be one of the most important survival skills for leaders and managers. Generally speaking, however, we are really not very good at working with our business models using systemic thinking. That is tough, conceptual, and analytical work that few are prepared for. At the same time it requires deep reflection on what it is we really want to do together and how we want to work.

Our challenge as workers, managers, and leaders is to identify the simplexities that will help us model and make sense of our interconnected, nonlinear, holonic, networked organizations. We need to learn how we can better self-organize to live on that creative edge of chaos.

This book offers a sampling of approaches and methods that will help us operate more effectively in a complex interdependent world. In particular, we have been exploring enterprise network patterns that we are now learning to make visible. Beneath these patterns we can find certain principles of behavior that are proving to be the helpful. Not surprisingly, many of these principles can also be found in life sciences as defining characteristics of healthy living systems.

EXCHANGE DYNAMICS

The natural processes of living systems are all based on some sort of exchange. Cells are in constant communication with each other, exchanging viruses, bacteria, loose snippets of DNA, water, etc. Our bodies are small universes of exchanges, with every part in communication, holding conversations with one another about the business of life. Exchange is the molecular level of value creation and the life process of the economy.

The Internet too is a vast web of conversations and exchanges. Human society weaves a rich social tapestry of conversations, interconnections, and exchanges—love, food, energy, knowledge, and stories. The daily exchanges of our lives reflect the exchanges of the ecosystems that sustain us, that in turn reflect the exchanges of the universe: energy, matter, and information.

Tangible Exchanges of Energy and Matter

People who have been studying complex systems find that ordered patterns emerge spontaneously in most networks, as long as there is a constant flow of energy and matter. In organizations, exchanges of energy and matter can be seen in the physical aspects of how the work gets done. Energy flows through the circuitry of our workplaces and through the digital highways of our financial system. I think of monetary transactions as a type of energy exchange. Matter also clearly flows through the tools and resources we need to do our work. We actively exchange matter in the form of products and services that we deliver to our customers and receive from our suppliers.

A value network analysis surfaces the patterns of such exchanges, but *not* with the linear process models and functional divisions that have dominated organizational design. We need to understand such exchanges in a nonlinear way that lets us see how all the material processes, functions, and roles work with each other. In this networked world of organizations, dynamic patterns of such exchanges at every level are more important than linear patterns.

Intangible Cognitive and Emotive Exchanges

We now know, too, that living systems also engage in cognitive processes and exchanges. In social systems, our patterns of knowledge exchange reveal the cognitive pathways and neural networks of collaborative or group intelligence. Social network analysis can reveal many of these patterns of organizational intelligence at work. When combined with a value network analysis, we make visible those patterns that are especially critical for building relationships and identify places where the cognitive pathways may need to be developed more or supported with technology.

Making intangible exchanges visible also helps us understand the emotive dynamics at work in a business or economic network. In humans, cognition and knowing are directly connected to feelings and emotions. Is it not possible that this is also true for organizations? We tend to speak of organizational knowledge and intelligence as if the organizational brain is somehow disconnected from the physical body of living, breathing humans with passions and emotions. But organizational intelligence is *human* intelligence, complete with feelings and desires.

Exchanges of knowledge and intangibles are intertwined with emotion to a much higher degree than are exchanges of goods, services, or revenue. Many times, favors and benefits have an emotive aspect that is essential for building trusting relationships. Knowledge cannot be separated from the conversations, relationships, and emotional fields from whence it emerges or transforms into new knowledge. We are emotionally connected to what we know, and when we extend knowledge to another we are extending ourselves. We engage with our full intelligence and our total being, even in the most ordinary of conversations.

Indeed, research has shown a strong connection between emotional intelligence and profitability. Emotional intelligence is a form of social intelligence that involves the ability to monitor one's own and another's feeling. Daniel Goleman, noted author on the topic, insists that "the single most important element in group intelligence, it turns out, is not the average IQ in the academic sense, but rather in terms of emotional intelligence."[1] The Levering and Moskowitz studies of great places to work also find that companies with excellent employee relationships and social harmony enjoy greater financial success than others in their industry.[2]

We used to address emotive issues under the guise of looking at organizational culture. Now, thanks to these researchers, a changing social climate, and the work in social capital addressed in Chapter 10, we can address interpersonal relationships and feelings more directly and appropriately in the workplace.

Knowledge cannot flourish where there is no trust. The fertile soil of good relationships allows bountiful harvests of creativity, innovation, and learning. Whenever we put processes before people, we lose these emotive aspects of organizational intelligence. Understanding organizations as living systems means putting people back into the picture as intelligent agents of action, fully capable of organizing in ways that support the vitality of the firm as well as personal success.

NEGOTIATED SELF-INTEREST

It is generally agreed in psychology that one milestone of maturity in individuals is when a person learns to temper personal needs for the sake of relationships and maintaining social order. We can see a similar maturation in the shifting values and ethics of business people toward socially and environmentally responsible business practices.

But there is something larger going on than just a philosophical shift. This type of behavior also signals the maturation of a living system. According to biologist Elisabet Sahtouris, author of *Earthdance*,[3] an important evolutionary milestone in living systems is when they begin to move from competition to cooperation. In a mature living system, every part, entity, or person pursues self-interest in a way that does not subvert the health of the whole.

At first glance, self-interest seems to be in direct opposition to a healthy system. The espoused "enlightened self-interest" of traditional economic and business behavior has been disastrous for the health of the environment and global society. Despite decades of charity, hand-outs, and good works, the economic gap between rich and poor has continued to widen, leaving millions to scramble for their daily food. Unchecked self-interest has resulted in plundered forests, pollution of all kinds, and squalid human conditions. Surely, we have had enough of self-interest!

The key, Sahtouris points out, lies in *negotiated* self-interest.[4] In a healthy family, the tension between personal self-interest and the collective is resolved through constant negotiation. There is recognition that the health and integrity of the family has its own self-interest. Sahtouris gives the example of couple-hood, a simple, two-level holarchy, where two individuals are not only negotiating with each other, but also with their couple-hood, the second level of the holoarchy. Maintaining the integrity and well-being of the couple-hood demands certain sacrifices of individual self-interest.

Most business decisions do not consider the health of other levels, or of other systems. The work demands of companies too often are made at the expense of families and communities. For the most part, we do not consider the health of other levels when using resources and materials such as local and global ecosystems. When all levels are able to express their needs and negotiate with the other levels, healthy, living systems are the result. They can successfully negotiate individual or local self-interest and group or global self-interest.

The first principle of a healthy network is that individual participants pursue negotiated self-interest with consideration of the health of the other levels of the system. The value network perspective and approach suggested in this book supports and encourages negotiated self-interest between all the participants, with careful consideration of the next level of holarchy—that of the value network itself. People will want others to succeed when they appreciate that their individual success is directly linked to the health and vitality of the entire network. In a successful value network, *everybody* supports the success of others as well as themselves.

Reciprocity and Fair Exchange

What we negotiate of course are exchanges. Every participant in a value network needs to contribute and receive tangible and intangible value in a way that sustains both their own success and that of the value network as a whole. When this does not happen, participants either withdraw or are expelled or the overall system becomes unstable and may collapse or reconfigure.

In the course of their negotiations, people need to feel they are being treated fairly. When people feel they are being fairly rewarded for the value they contribute, they become willing to offer even more value. I think of this as the principle of fair exchange or reciprocity. It is essential that everyone in the network operate with an ethic of giving and receiving value in a way that builds good relationships and trust.

Remember the simple philosophy of Sergio Lub, mentioned in Chapter 13. The happiest people are those who give. "The more one gives, the more others give and there are suddenly more apples on the tree to eat." When there is a climate of fair exchange, it creates a positive reinforcing loop that leads to more value, more abundance, more trusting relationships, and more prosperity.

Self-Organization

Negotiated self-interest is the way a living system manages itself. A truly complex system, such as an organization, cannot be designed or engineered from the outside to make it work well. There are simply too many variables. For decades, we have tried to manage our organizations from the outside in, by designing structures, systems, rules, and formal reporting relationships. Now, many such efforts seem to get in the way more than they help.

The only way a complex system can be healthy is if it is allowed to work "from the inside out" through self-organization. The concept of

An Example of Self-Organization

Let's take a business example of self-organization. A company can have a guiding principle of providing superior customer service. If people are allowed sufficient autonomy to interpret that principle, then an infinite variety of customer situations can be met with superb service. If that principle becomes too rule-bound and complicated, the system becomes inflexible and customer service actually declines. As a customer, you have undoubtedly encountered both environments and probably prefer the system that gives the service person guidelines, authority, and flexibility to directly respond to your request.

self-organization originated from early studies regarding the logic inherent in neural networks, such as the brain. Complex adaptive systems, including living systems, exhibit behavior that is orderly enough to be stable, but flexible enough to adapt to the environment.

For self-organization to happen, there must be autonomous agents, such as people, who don't behave quite the same way under the same conditions, so their exact behavior can never be predicted; yet, the rules that guide behavior must necessarily be simple. That very simplicity is what creates the freedom and flexibility to act in different ways. Self-organization allows spontaneous emergence of new structures and new forms of behaviors.

Self-organizing more accurately should be called selves organizing—each individual self-organizing according to their own interests, with consideration of the health of the system that supports it. The core activity of a healthy value network is not competition, nor is it complete cooperation, as some would have us believe. It is true *negotiation*, in the moment, every moment, everywhere, by everyone.

So where is the center? The center is where *you* are! In a healthy living system or organization, everyone pursues his or her self-interest *with consideration* of the other participants, of the whole system, and of the other levels of holarchy. That does not mean operating under the direction *of* the system; it means being an autonomous participant *in* the system, working for the health and vitality of oneself and the greater good.

IT'S ALL ABOUT RELATIONSHIPS

The value network perspective makes it abundantly clear that success today is all about relationships. We sometimes are dazzled by technologies and what they can enable us to do. But the bottom line is that business is about exchanges and transactions that happen between *real people*. Even when people never see each other or speak directly, only *real people* can make decisions and initiate action. Technologies may fill the role of decision-makers at times, but only based on what a real person would do.

When business is viewed as a linear process, a set of functions, or simply material transactions, it not only diminishes the role of people, it makes invisible the all-important human relationships. The value network focus puts people back into the business model in such a way that they can see who they need to be in relationship with and what their responsibility is in that relationship.

It is entirely possible to have business relationships with almost no intangible value being exchanged or generated. However, enduring business relationships are rarely built solely on tangible transactions, especially when dealing with sophisticated or complex products and services. The value network view demonstrates that knowledge and intangibles build the critical business relationships and create the environment for business success. We do not so much build a business but rather grow or "weave" a web of trusted relationships.

Companies and organizations that build healthy and rewarding relationships usually find they have engaged in intangible exchanges for months, or even years, before the tangible activities kick off with an order or a request for service. Once intangibles become visible, people can easily define their importance in building good relationships, and they are more willing to invest resources in producing and delivering them.

Integrity Is not an Option

One of the hallmarks of systems thinking is respect. Whole-system awareness brings humility and genuine respect for the system we are working with as well as for the limitations of our own understanding. It is easy to assume we know more that we do and that we are smarter than we really are. We hurry to fix one part of the system only to find another part jumps up and bites us. Respecting the integrity of the whole is not an option; it is one of the new fundamentals of systemic thinking.

Integrity of the Whole

In every system, the whole is greater than the sum of its parts. This means a single transaction, even a group of transactions, is only meaningful in relationship with the value network as a whole. A single participant is only meaningful in relationship with the other participants.

Living networks are so interdependent that the removal of a single node or relationship can reverberate through the whole network. Removing a key participant or critical transaction can affect the value dynamics across an entire enterprise or business web. Breaking an operating principle, assumption, or agreement, implied or explicit, can destroy the integrity of the whole system, turning positive reinforcing loops into negative ones. A living system dies when its pattern of organization has been destroyed.

Integrity of the Participant

One participant cannot manage a whole system. Not even all participants working together can really "manage" the system, even through

agreed behaviors and values. However, for maximum benefit all the participants need to understand how the whole system is working, so they can fully participate, gain the greatest value, yet help maintain the integrity of the whole.

Participants must understand network principles so they can manage their own inputs and outputs in ways that support the vitality of the whole value network. Every individual must learn the art of negotiated self-interest. In order to negotiate intelligently, people need ways to identify and leverage the value gained from every tangible or intangible they receive. Further, each participant must find ways to enhance or increase the value of what they are contributing to other participants and to the value network as a whole.

Fair exchange is an essential element for a healthy value network. Knowledge and other intangible exchanges become richer and more frequent where there is trust. Trust widens the pipeline. If people don't trust each other, they don't exchange knowledge and ideas and are reluctant to extend favors. When people are treated fairly and can trust the other members of their networks and organizations, they are far more likely to fully participate and make their greatest contributions. Everyone has the responsibility for maintaining the highest possible personal integrity to build the climate of trust.

Integrity of the Leader

These new network fundamentals are driving business leaders to higher levels of integrity and fairness than ever were required in the past. In the digital world there are no secrets and corporate leadership is becoming increasingly transparent. In the old competitive environment, a business could treat one external partner badly and still be successful. Today, such behaviors erode the entire web of relationships. While many business executives continue to operate by industrial-age competitive values, we can anticipate that the most successful companies of the future will be those that honor relationships and embrace the ethics of honesty and fair exchange.

The Prosperity Potential

I began this book by suggesting that an intangibles–based economy offers a far better foundation for prosperity than one based only on tangible and monetary value. Money is a commodity that is controlled by only a relatively few members of society. Knowledge and favors are within the power of everyone to create, distribute, and exchange. In the right climate of trust, positive reinforcement fuels a continuing cycle of intangible wealth creation.

There is no need to overthrow the old economic order to usher in a new abundance. We did not overthrow agriculture when we moved to an industrial economy; it was absorbed into a new economic order. We will continue to include money and tangibles in the range of things we might negotiate. But with intangibles we expand our economic possibilities and opportunities.

Tangibles operate by the laws of physics. They have their own laws and dynamics that we are quite familiar with. Intangibles operate by the law of social value, and we are only now learning their true role and contribution to value creation. I anticipate that our business understanding will evolve to a larger perspective and a new economic synthesis, one that understands all of these exchanges from an expanded worldview. Right now, our questions about intangibles are anomalies that we do not understand quite yet. But as we pursue our questions, they will serve as the gateway to our future knowledge.

Conclusion

In this book we have traced the future of knowledge along several dimensions.

- We explored how our business knowledge is evolving to the next level of complexity so that we may learn to see, understand, and work with complex systems and network dynamics.

- We have reviewed some of the new tools and methods that are helping us improve and apply collective intelligence in our business settings. We are acknowledging that knowledge is a social process that emerges in and travels through networks, communities, and webs of conversations.
- We have considered how the Internet is enabling the natural network pattern of organizations to emerge as new forms of enterprise, network organizations, business webs, and economic clusters.
- We have seen the economic future of knowledge as an intangible asset, negotiable, and deliverable that can be leveraged to create value and usher in a new prosperity.

Living systems and complexity theory offer up a rich array of principles and network dynamics that are essential for understanding the role of knowledge in value creation, in communities, and in organizations. Not everyone agrees that organizations are living systems, or that social systems behave like living systems. Many of these concepts are controversial when applied to business. As we struggle to understand network dynamics and the changing world of enterprise, we can anticipate lively debate, false starts, and dead ends. On the other hand, we will also experience some amazing breakthroughs as true systems thinking becomes more familiar and we develop new managerial tools.

Any business modeling approach has limitations. But in today's complex business environment, where competitive advantage often rises from innovations and relationships, a network perspective is the foundation for helping people address complex systemic issues in organizations, business webs, and economic webs. As our understanding increases, we will be able to work more deliberately with our models—not only with the physical aspects, but with the intangible aspects as well, including emotive exchanges that forge real relationships and open us to the creative in each other. With that understanding, we can more consciously evolve the systems, structures, values, and relationships that will lead us to a more hopeful future.

Chapter Endnotes

[1] Daniel Goleman, *Emotional Intelligence,* Bantam Books, 1995.

[2] Robert Levering and Milton Moskowitz, *The 100 Best Companies to Work For*, Fortune, February 4, 2000.

[3] Elisabet Sahtouris and James Lovelock, *Earthdance: Living Systems in Evolution,* Universe.com, 2000.

[4] Elisabet Sahtouris, "Living Systems, The Internet and Human Future," presentation, Planetwork, Global Ecology and Information Technology, San Francisco, May 2000. Available at www.sahtouris.com.

© *2002 Hemera Technologies Inc.*

Relationships are all there is. Everything in the universe only exists because it is in relationship to everything else.

—Meg Wheatley

FIFTEEN
Reflections

In the past, we have addressed our business problems at the material level and at the behavioral level. At the material level, we learned to work with physical objects in the production line and created financial abstractions as a symbolic language to represent the material world. In the second half of the twentieth century, we began to approach business problems at the behavioral level, looking at team dynamics, organizational behavior, and leadership.

We are now beginning to approach business challenges at the cognitive level and, more particularly, as issues involving social cognition and collaborative intelligence. Organizational learning questions first opened the door, and the knowledge questions have deepened our focus on the cognitive approach. Our questions of learning and knowledge are now opening our awareness to three other aspects of organizational cognition.

The first level has to do with patterns of relationships—systemic learning that explores dynamic relationships and patterns in systems, including thought patterns in our shared inner world and emerging creations. The second level concerns the emotive aspects of knowledge sharing and intelligence that are becoming legitimate management topics, as we seek to create more trusting and collaborative work environments. Finally, we are also acknowledging a deeper level of social cognition or knowing that arises from a sense of our role in the natural order of things as co-creators of the world and as intelligent agents for the creative expression of life itself. Let's consider this third level.

Self-Creation

Organizations are social systems that form around shared beliefs, values, identity, and purpose. Our sense of who we are and what we are about evolves into structures and relationships that help us maintain our identity and purpose. We do this as individuals, as organizations, and as whole societies and nation states. Our character and purpose attract others who resonate with our identity, purpose, and values and who will help maintain them.

As intelligent, autopoietic systems, all organizations—or, rather, the people they comprise—have the capacity to perpetuate and to renew themselves without losing their identity or basic pattern of organization. We can do this because we collectively have awareness of ourselves as a social group. People working together have a sense of themselves as a group or community, easily identifying those who are "one of us" and those who are not.

Since we are individually aware of ourselves as a "self," we can reflect on our sense of identity and the values and beliefs that guide us to certain behaviors. We can mentally place ourselves in different scenarios and role-play different identities to explore alternative pathways and actions. We can reflect on our communities and businesses, considering different possibilities for our existence and our future.

So, not only can we analyze the results of our past actions, we can project into the future and consider the possible outcomes of any number of potential actions. This gives us an enormous range of possible responses and is one of the reasons we have proven to be so successful (so far) as a species.

Our ability to mentally step outside ourselves, outside time, and outside space, gives us the creative capacity to continually redefine ourselves and the organizations we create. We can collectively consider our own interests and the interests of every other level of holarchy if we so choose. This capacity gives us the ability to take intelligent actions through negotiated self-interest that work for the health and well-being of all. But these are conscious choices and only our collective will determines which path we will choose.

A WORLD EMERGES

Both our present understanding of the world and our projections into the future arise through a social process of knowing. As was pointed out in Chapter 9, it is imperative that we have a better understanding of how we form a shared social reality that shapes our perception, thinking, and actions. This is the greatest cognitive or knowledge challenge of all. How do we work more deliberately with the social realities that emerge and form through conversations and shape the world we create?

In Gestalt psychology, people refer to the foreground and the background. The foreground is what we can see or observe, what is visible. The background is the matrix or ground from which whatever is in the foreground emerges. As a metaphor for thinking about organizations, we can think of the systems that we create and participate in, such as organizations, as the foreground or the *outer world*. They emerge out of the matrix, background, or *inner world* of our shared assumptions and beliefs. The social and physical aspects of the outer world in turn shape our collective experience and understanding (see Figure 15.1). Ours is not a static world, but one constantly in motion.

FIGURE 15.1 *The inner world of our shared social reality shapes the outer world that we create.*

Conscious conversation helps us fine-tune our ability to make meaning together, to sense our way into systems understanding, and to work directly with our cognitive processes. The pace of these deeper explorations tends to be much slower, as we engage more fully with each other. Slowing down allows space to open—in the in-between places between the thoughts. Developing this contemplative capacity moves us from communal learning and everyday problem solving into the larger internal and creative spaces. There we are able to see whole-system patterns and tap into our deeper wisdom and knowing. The quiet places are where the dreams emerge that will shape our future.

We dream the world together and it reflects back to us what we have envisioned. If we would change our outer world of business and organizations, then together we also must learn to collectively attend to our beliefs about what should be and what is possible. We need to learn to share our values, emotions, desires, and wishes in conversation with others about questions that matter. Full intelligence requires our full being and presence to listen to each other.

Being the playful, creative, thinking creatures humans are, we manifest our thoughts into form and expression. We experiment. We create systems, products, technologies, organizations, and cultures that shape us as we shape them in return. People exploring shared questions form patterns of collective thought and belief and create patterns of relationship and interaction. Together, we reflect on our work and then think together once again. The better we can see and understand our organizations with a whole-system perspective, the more likely we will be to create healthy workplaces that are good for business, good for people, and good for the planet.

We come together in purposeful organizations to manifest our dreams. An endless, creative cycle turns as we dream, create, experiment, and then dream again. Philosopher Lao-Tse wonders, "Am I a man dreaming I am a butterfly, or a butterfly dreaming I am a man?" In the living world of organizations we might ask, "Do our beliefs shape the systems we create, or do the systems we participate in shape what we believe to be possible?" In the continuing cycle of knowing, believing, and creation, perhaps the answer to both questions is simply—yes.

APPENDIX
The Knowledge
Complexity Archetype

Archetypes are basic human ways of organizing. They help us understand our experience and find our common humanity. We continually rediscover archetypes over time. Every culture and era seems to discover them anew.

Familiar geometric archetypes are squares, triangles, and circles. Design and architecture incorporate these elements all over the world. They often show up as teaching devices or models as well. Psychological archetypes surface in stories such as the hero's journey, and in fundamental social structures such as the relationship between mother and child. Archetypes communicate at fundamental psychological and cognitive levels.

The Knowledge Archetype is a basic organizing structure that surfaces repeatedly in discussions of knowledge and complexity. It correlates to theories of brain development, such as those of Paul MacLean. He suggests that as we have evolved as a species, we have developed far beyond the basic instinctual processes of the "reptilian" lower brain. Our middle brain, or "mammalian" brain, processes input at the more emotional level. The outer brain, the neocortex, handles abstract thinking. The neocortex is figuratively our "thinking cap" of abstract reasoning.[1]

---

1 Paul D. MacLean, *A Triune Concept of Brain and Behavior* (Toronto: University of Toronto Press, 1973).

The *Knowledge Complexity Framework* (see Figure A.1) visually depicts the knowledge archetype. Every aspect of knowing is interdependent on the others in our universe of knowing. It is important to understand this quality *of embeddedness.* That means these are not discrete levels but rather way-stations along a continuum of complexity. The more variables we are processing, the more complex the cognitive task. At greater levels of abstraction, knowledge work becomes more challenging, increasingly collaborative and social in nature.

Since the modes are on a continuum of increasing complexity and integration, there are different learning, information processing, and knowledge processing dynamics for each one. Each aspect of knowledge or knowing has a corresponding learning activity that supports it. Since learning is demonstrated by improved performance, each learn-

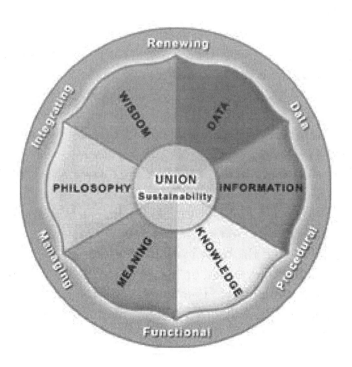

FIGURE A.1   *Knowledge Complexity Framework. (© 1994 Verna Allee.)*

ing mode supports a different performance focus. Each knowledge and action focus is also associated with a time horizon and with a particular mode of attention or consciousness (see Table A.1).

TABLE A.1   *Knowledge Complexity Framework Reference Chart*

KNOWLEDGE Learning	ACTION FOCUS Performance Goal
DATA Instinctual learning	DATA Feedback
Sensing. The data mode of learning is at the sensory or input level. Little actual learning takes place.	*Gathering information.* Receiving input, registering data and variations without reflection.
Time perspective: Immediate moment Consciousness: Awareness	
INFORMATION Single-Loop learning	PROCEDURAL Efficiency
Action without reflection. Procedural learning entails redirecting a course of action to follow a predetermined course. Learning is mostly trial and error.	*Doing something the most efficient way.* Conforming to standards or making simple adjustments and modifications. Focus is on developing and following and completing tasks.
Time perspective: Very short (present—*now*) Consciousness: Physical sentience	
KNOWLEDGE Double-Loop learning	FUNCTIONAL Effectiveness
Self-conscious reflection. A larger perspective that involves evaluation and modification of the goal or objective as well as design of the path or procedures used to get there. Learning requires self-conscious reflection.	*Doing it the best way.* Evaluating and choosing between two or more alternative paths. Goals are effective action and resolution of inconsistencies. Focus is on effective work design and engineering aspects, such as process redesign.
Time perspective: Short (immediate past and present) Consciousness: Self-reflective	

TABLE A.1 (continued)

MEANING	MANAGING
Communal learning	Productivity
Understanding context, relationships, and trends. Learning requires the making of meaning, which includes understanding context or "the story," seeing trends, and generating alternatives. Variables considered are relationships between components as well as comprehending roles and relationships between people.	*Understanding what promotes or impedes effectiveness.* Effective management and allocation of resources and tasks, using conceptual frameworks to analyze and track multiple variables. Encompasses planning and measuring results. Also attends to working roles, relationships, and culture.

Time perspective: Medium to long (historic past, present, very near future)

Consciousness: Communal

PHILOSOPHY	INTEGRATING
Deutero Learning	Optimization
Self-organizing. Integrative or systemic learning seeks to understand dynamic relationships and nonlinear processes, discerning the patterns that connect, including archetypes and metaphors. Requires recognition of the embeddedness and interdependence of systems.	*Seeing where an activity fits the whole picture.* Understanding and managing sociocultural system dynamics. Focus is on the ability to adapt to a changing environment. Comprises long-range forecasting, development of multilevel strategies, and evaluating investments and policies with regard to long-term success.

Time perspective: Long-term (past, present, and future)
Consciousness: Pattern

WISDOM	RENEWING
Generative Learning	Integrity
Value driven. Learning for the joy of learning, in open interaction with the environment. It involves creative processes; heuristic, open-ended explorations; and profound self-questioning. Allows for the discovery of one's highest capabilities and talents, purpose, and intentions.	*Finding or reconnecting with one's purpose.* Defining or reconnecting with values, vision, and mission. Understanding purpose. Very long-term time frame leads to deep awareness of ecology, community, and ethical action.

Time perspective: Very long-term (very distant past to far distant future)
Consciousness: Ethical

TABLE A.1 (continued)

UNION Synergistic	UNION Sustainability
Connection. Learning integrates direct experience and appreciation of oneness or deep connection with the greater cosmos. Requires contemplative processes that connect personal and collective purpose to the health and well-being of the larger community and the environment.	*Understanding values in greater context.* Intergenerational time perspective evokes commitment to the greater good of society, the environment, and the planet. Performance is demonstrated in actions consistent with these deeper values.

Time perspective: Intergenerational, timeless
Consciousness: Universal

THEORETICAL FOUNDATIONS OF THE KNOWLEDGE COMPLEXITY ARCHETYPE

The theoretical discussion of the Knowledge Complexity Archetype can be found in Appendix 1 of *The Knowledge Evolution: Expanding Organizational Intelligence.* Included is a comparative table of models and notes on various theorists exploring some aspect of human consciousness, intelligence, organizational learning, organizational knowledge, or managerial complexity. Included in the discussion are:

- Peter Senge, five disciplines
- Nonaka and Takeuchi, knowledge conversion
- Dorothy Leonard, dimensions of core capabilities
- Erich Jantsch, managerial focus
- Stafford Beer, viable systems model
- Elliott Jacques, stratified systems
- Russell Ackoff, knowledge continuum
- W. Edwards Deming, quality philosophy
- Stuart Hart, strategy processes
- Abraham Maslow, hierarchy of needs
- Lawrence Kohlberg, moral development

- Jean Piaget, cognitive development
- Arthur Young, theory of process
- Yogic Philosophy, mind and energy
- Ken Wilber, levels of consciousness
- Sharon Franquemont, intuition inspiral
- Howard Gardner, multiple intelligences
- Gareth Morgan, organizational models
- Peter Koestenbaum, organizational intelligence

Glossary of Terms

Action Review
A systematic learning debrief that takes place at key milestones during a project or after a critical incident.

Autopoietic Network
A network that continually reproduces itself through a cognitive process so that being and doing are inseparable. This term and the process related to it, autopoiesis, are taken from the work of Humberto Maturana and Francisco Varela.[1]

Business Model
A set of rules and relationships that describe how a business operates and creates value.

Business Relationship Capital
The quality of alliances and business relationships with customers, strategic partners, suppliers, investors, regulatory bodies, and government groups.

Business Web
Partner networks of producers, service providers, suppliers, infrastructure companies, and customers, usually linked via digital channels.

Chaord

Term adopted by the Chaordic Alliance, founded by Dee Hock who launched VISA. Defined as (1) any autocatalytic, self-regulating, adaptive, nonlinear, complex organism, organization, or system, whether physical, biological or social, the behavior of which harmoniously exhibits characteristics of both order and chaos; (2) an entity whose behavior exhibits patterns and probabilities not governed or explained by the behavior of its parts; (3) the fundamental organizing principle of nature and evolution.

Cognition

The act or process of knowing, including aspects such as awareness, perception, reason, judgment, and impetus to action.

Communal Learning

Organizational learning or group learning that requires the making of meaning, which involves understanding context, seeing trends, detecting relationships among components, determining roles and relationships between people, and generating and choosing alternative paths to reach a goal.

Community of Practice

A group or network of individuals who share a concern, a set of problems, or a passion about a topic, and who deepen their knowledge and expertise in this area by interacting with each other on an ongoing basis (taken from Wenger, McDermott, and Snyder).[2]

Complex Adaptive System

A system that exhibits complex nonlinear behavior and adapts to the environment.

Complexity Theory

An umbrella term that refers to the interdisciplinary exploration of a set of theories from different fields, all of which share focus on complex adaptive systems and evolution.

Culture
The pattern of beliefs, knowledge, attitudes, norms of behaviors, and customs that exist in an organization.

Customer Capital
See Business Relationship Capital.

Deliverable
A deliverable can be a tangible product or service (e.g., a pair of jeans or a manicure). It can also be an intangible product (e.g., information or knowledge about something), or an intangible benefit (e.g., political support that one person can bestow or give to another).

Deutero Learning
Second-order learning that demonstrates the capacity to reflect on and inquire into previous contexts for learning—in other words, to think and learn systemically.

Dissipative Structures
Systems that are sustained by the persistent dissipation of matter and energy.

Double Loop Learning
The ability to reflect on one's actions, choose alternatives, and modify one's behavior.

Emotional Intelligence
A form of social intelligence that involves the ability to monitor one's own and other's feelings.

Environmental Capital or Environmental Success
The value of one's relationship with the earth and its resources, as understood through calculation of the true costs of resources consumed by an enterprise or economy and determination of equitable exchange or contribution to the health and sustainability of the environment.

Exchange
Two or more transactions between different people or groups of people, with a quality of reciprocity (e.g., an exchange of money for service).

Exchange Analysis
An assessment of overall patterns and system dynamics of value exchange, to determine whether the value-creating system is healthy, sustainable, and expanding.

Explicit Knowledge
Knowledge that is codified and conveyed to others through dialog, demonstration, or media such as books, drawings, and documents.

External Structure
See Business Relationship Capital.

General Systems Theory
A comprehensive theoretical framework describing the principles of organization of living systems.

Generative Learning
Value-driven learning that seeks what is alive, compelling, and energizing and that expresses a willingness to see radical possibilities beyond the boundaries of current thinking.

Goodwill
Historically, goodwill has been considered as the positive disposition of a customer towards a particular enterprise. Components of goodwill, however, include any consideration of the company or its management that causes people to hold it in high regard.

Holonic Organization
A pattern of organization in which like objects, organisms, or systems nest with and within other like systems.

HoloMapping®
A systems mapping technique that shows the key transactions between participants in a system.

Human Capital
See Human Competence.

Human Competence
Individual capabilities, knowledge, skills, experience, and problem-solving abilities that reside in people.

Identity (Corporate or Organizational)
The vision, purpose, values, ethical stance, character, and leadership qualities that contribute to brand and economic success in business and employee relationships.

Impact Analysis
An assessment of the tangible and intangible costs (or risks), and tangible and intangible gains of value inputs.

Intangible Assets
Those nonphysical factors and resources under some degree of control that are critical for the present or future success of the business and that do not show up on the financial balance sheet.

Intellectual Capital
Another term for intangible assets that includes any knowledge or qualities of value for an organization.

Intellectual Property
Intellectual capital over which the firm enjoys a legally protected owner's interest, such as patents, trademarks, copyrights, registered design, and trade secrets.

Internal Structure
Infrastructure, routines, concepts, models, information systems, work systems, and business processes that support productivity and that stay behind in an organization when its employees go home, including IT,

communication technologies, systems and software, databases, documents, images, concepts and models of how the business operates, patents, copyrights and other codified knowledge.

Intangible Deliverables

Knowledge and benefits extended or delivered by a person or group, that are noncontractual but still have value to the recipient.

Intangible Value

Value generated by informal, noncontractual activities that help build business relationships and contribute to operational effectiveness.

Knowledge

The state of knowing. Variously defined in the knowledge management field as *the capacity to act* and *the process of knowing*. Also, familiarity, awareness, or understanding gained through experience or study.

Knowledge Artifacts

An artifact is something created for a practical purpose. In a work environment, a knowledge artifact might be a document, a process, a body of source code for a software program, an engineering schematic, or a template for a proposal, among other things.

Knowledge Assets

See Intangible Assets.

Knowledge Management

The facilitation and support of processes for creating, sustaining, sharing, and renewing of organizational knowledge in order to generate economic wealth, create value, or improve performance.

Learning

The process of gaining knowledge or skill or developing a behavior through study, instruction, or experience.

Learning Organization
An organization that is able to adapt to change and move forward successfully by acquiring new knowledge, skills, or behaviors, thereby transforming itself.

Network
A pattern of organization that is a set of nonlinear, nonhierarchical relationships that nest with other networks.

Organization
A complex, adaptive social system that forms around shared purpose, beliefs, and guiding principles that influence decisions, relationships, and human behavior.

Organizational Intelligence
The cognitive capacities and capabilities of an organization.

Organizational Knowledge
The accumulated know-how, expertise, and ways of working identified with a particular organization that become so embedded in the physical and social systems that the knowledge essentially remains accessible to the organization, even if key individuals leave.

Organizational Learning
Activities or processes whereby an organization exercises its collective ability to make sense of its environment and respond with more adaptive behaviors.

Organizational Structure
The set of essential defining characteristics of the enterprise that describe its physical embodiment as an organization.

Outsourcing
The practice of subcontracting certain business activities to outside companies.

Paradigm
A set of assumptions, concepts, values, and practices that constitutes a way of viewing reality for the community that shares them, particularly as it pertains to an intellectual discipline.

Participants (in a value network)
Real people or groups of people that generate transactions, send messages, engage in interactions, conduct processes, create value, and make decisions. They can be individuals, groups or subgroups, organizations, collectives or aggregates, communities, or nation-states.

Process
(1) A series of actions, changes, or functions bringing about a result. (2) A natural, continuing activity or function (such as breathing or cognition).

Prosperity
The condition of being successful; thriving.

Self-Organization
The spontaneous emergence of new structures and new forms of behaviors in open systems far from equilibrium, characterized by internal feedback loops.

Simplexity
Simple patterns of relationships and principles that help in understanding or modeling complexity. Simplexities describe foundational elements of a complex situation or system.

Social Capital
Traditional meaning: features of social organizations such as networks, norms, and social trust, that facilitate coordination and cooperation for mutual benefit. More recently: consists of the stock of active connections among people—the trust, mutual understanding, and shared values and behaviors that bind the members of human networks and communities and make cooperative action possible.[3]

Social Citizenship Capital

The quality and value of relationships enjoyed with larger society through the exercise of corporate citizenship as a member of local, regional and global communities.

Social Network Analysis

A social science discipline that focuses on relationships among social entities, such as members of a group, within or between organizations or nations. It explores both directional and bidirectional exchanges, including sharing of information or business relationships.

Structural Capital

See Internal Structure.

System

A whole that cannot be divided into independent parts without losing the integrity of the whole and losing the integrity of the parts.

Systemic Learning

See Deutero Learning.

Systems Thinking

A way of thinking about and describing the forces and interrelationships that shape the behavior of systems.

Tacit Knowledge

Deeply personal experiences, aptitudes, perceptions, insights, and know-how that are implied or indicated but not actually expressed.

Tangible Assets

Those assets that show up on the financial balance sheet, such as cash reserves, physical property, machinery, and accounts receivable.

Tangible Value

Value that is generated by contractual activities that contribute directly to economic gain.

Transaction
An activity generated by a person that involves conveying a tangible or intangible product, service, or benefit to another person.

Value Creation Analysis
An assessment of the tangible and intangible costs and gains for each value output that each participant contributes to a value network.

Value Chain
Another term for the core business process.

Value Network
A web of relationships that generates tangible and intangible value through complex, dynamic exchanges between individuals, groups, or organizations. Any organization or group of organizations, engaged in both tangible and intangible exchanges, can be viewed as a value network, whether private industry, government, or the public sector.

ValueNet Works™ **Analysis**
A whole-systems mapping and analysis approach to understanding tangible and intangible value creation among participants in an enterprise system.

Wealth
Traditional—An abundance of valuable material possessions or resources.
True—the condition or state of well-being and potential value expressed as economic, social, and environmental health and vitality.

Whole-System Theory or Thinking
See Systems Thinking.

Worldview
A core set of beliefs and principles by which people cognitively organizes and interprets their sensory, emotional, and mental experiences.

CHAPTER ENDNOTES

[1] Humberto R Maturana and Francisco J Varela, *The Tree of Knowledge: The Biological Roots of Human Understanding*, Shambala, 1987.

[2] Etienne Wenger, Richard McDermott, and William M Snyder, *Cultivating Communities of Practice: A Guide to Managing Knoweldge*, Harvard Business School Press, 2002.

[3] Laurence Prusak and Don Cohen, *In Good Company: How Social Capital Makes Organizations Work*, Harvard Business School Press, 2001.

Bibliography

Accenture.com, "Grasping the Capability: Successful Alliance Creation and Governance Through the Connected Corporation: Executive Summary," as of March 11, 2002.

Allee, Verna. "Evolving Business Forms for the Knowledge Economy." *The Handbook of Knowledge Management*, Clyde W Holsapple, Ed., Springer-Verlas, 2002.

Allee, Verna. "Knowledge Networks and Communities of Practice." *Organizational Development Practitioner*, Fall-Winter 2000.

Allee, Verna. "Reconfiguring the Value Network." *Journal of Business Strategy*, July-August 2000.

Allee, Verna. "The Art and Practice of Being a Revolutionary." *Journal of Knowledge Management*, MCB University Press, Vol 3, No 2, 1999.

Allee, Verna. "The Value Evolution: Addressing Larger Implications of an Intellectual Capital and Intangibles Perspective." *Journal of Intellectual Capital*, MCB University Press, Vol 1, No 1, 2000.

Allee, Verna. *The Knowledge Evolution: Expanding Organizational Intelligence.* Butterworth-Heinemann, 1997.

Armstrong, Charles, and Valdis Krebs. "Knowledge Networks: We Are our Artefacts (sic)." *HIRIM Journal*, October-December 2000.

Arthur, Brian. "Increasing Returns and the New World of Business." *Harvard Business Review*, July/Aug 1996.

Author Unknown. "Treasures Revealed." *CFO Magazine*, April 2001.

Bateson, Gregory. *Steps to An Ecology of Mind.* New York: Ballentine, 1972, pp 166–176.

Bernasek, Anna. "The Productivity Miracle is For Real." *Fortune*, March 18, 2002.

Blair, Margaret M, and Steven MH Wallman. *Unseen Wealth: Report of the Brookings Task Force on Intangibles.* Brookings Institution Press, 2001.

Bohm, David. *Wholeness and the Implicate Order.* ARK, 1980, 1983.

Boisot, Max. *Information Space: A Framework for Learning in Organizations, Institutions and Culture.* Routledge, 1995.

Boisot, Max. *Knowledge Assets: Securing Competitive Advantage in the Knowledge Economy.* Oxford University Press, 1998.

Brandenberger, Adam M, Jerry L Nalebuff, and Ada Brandenberger. *Co-opetition: 1. A Revolutionary Mindset That Redefines Competition and Cooperation; 2. The Game Theory Strategy That's Changing the Game of Business.* Doubleday, 1997.

Brown, John Seely, and Paul Duguid. *The Social Life of Information.* Harvard Business School Press, 2000.

Brown, Juanita, and David Issacs. "Conversation as a Core Business Process." *The Systems Thinker*, Vol 7, No 10, December 1996.

Brown, Juanita, David Issacs, and The World Café Community, "The World Café: Living Knowledge Through Conversations that Matter," *The Systems Thinker*, Vol 12, No 5, June/July 2001.

Brown, Juanita. *The World Café: Living Knowledge Through Conversations that Matter.* PhD Dissertation, The Fielding Institute, 2001. Available through www.theworldcafe.com.

Brown, Shona L, and Kathleen M Eisenhardt. *Competing on the Edge: Strategy as Structured Chaos.* Harvard Business School Press, 2001.

Brownmiller, Susan. "The eBay Obsession." *My Generation*, May-June, 2002.

Caldwell, French. "Creating Resiliency with the E-Workplace." Gartner, Inc., 03 January, 2002.

Capra, Fritjof. *The Web of Life, A New Scientific Understanding of Living Systems.* Anchor Books, 1996.

Carter, Barry C. *Infinite Wealth: A New World of Collaboration and Abundance in the Knowledge Era.* Butterworth-Heinemann, 1999.

CIO.com. "B2B Commerce to Eclipse $4 trillion by 2005." *CIO.com,* November 2001. www.cio.com.

Clippinger, John Henry III, Editor. *The Biology of Business: Decoding the Natural Laws of Enterprise.* San Francisco: Jossey-Bass, 1999.

Cohen, Don, and Laurence Prusak. *In Good Company: How Social Capital Makes Organizations Work.* Harvard Business School Press, 2001.

Coleman, David. "Distributed Project Management Comes of Age." *www.collaborate.com,* 2000. www.collaborate.com.

Collison, Chris, and Geoff Parcell. *Learning to Fly: How BP Became One of the World's Leading Knowledge Companies.* New York: John Wiley & Sons, 2001.

Cross, Rob. "More Than an Answer: How Seeking Information Facilitates Knowledge Creation and Use." *IBM Institute of Knowledge Management,* September 2000.

Cross, Rob, Nitin Norhia, and Andrew Parker. "Six Myths about Informal Networks and How to Overcome Them." *MIT Sloan Management Review,* Spring 2002.

Dannemiller Tyson Associates. *Whole-Scale Change: Unleashing the Magic in Organizations.* Berrett-Koehler, 2000.

Davidow, William H, and Michael S Malone. *The Virtual Corporation: Structuring and Revitalizing the Corporation for the 21st Century.* Harper Business, 1992.

Dawson, Ross. *Developing Knowledge-Based Client Relationships: The Future of Professional Services.* Butterworth-Heinemann, 2000.

Deloitte and Touche Tohmatsu. *Corporate Environmental Report Score Card.* Deloitte & Touche, 1997.

Denning, Stephen. *The Springboard: How Storytelling Ignites Action in Knowledge-Era Organizations.* Butterworth-Heinemann, 2001.

Dialogonleadership.org. "Grasping the Capability: Successful Alliance Creation and Governance Through the Connected Corporation: Executive Summary." *dialogonleadership.org,* as of March 11, 2002. www.dialogonleadership.org.

DiBella, Anthony J, and Edwin C Nevis. *How Organizations Learn: An Integrated Strategy for Building Learning Capability.* San Francisco: Jossey-Bass, 1998.

Dixon, Nancy M. *Common Knowledge: How Companies Thrive by Sharing What They Know.* Harvard Business School Press, 2000.

Drucker, Peter F. *Post-Capitalist Society.* Harper Business, 1993.

Edvinsson, Leif, and Michael Malone. *Intellectual Capital: Realizing Your Company's True Value by Finding its Hidden Brainpower.* New York: Harper Business, 1997.

Faithorn, Lisa and Kathleen Cody. "Helpline Core Service Evaluation Final Report." O'Neil and Associates, 1999.

Geus, Arie de. *The Living Company: Habits for Survival in a Turbulent Business Environment.* Boston: Harvard Business School Press, 1997.

Goleman, Daniel. *Emotional Intelligence.* Bantam Books, 1995.

Hampton-Turner, Charles. *Charting the Corporate Mind: Graphic Solutions to Business Conflicts.* Free Press, 1990.

Helgersen, Sally. *The Web of Inclusion: A New Architecture for Building Great Organizations.* Currency/Doubleday, 1995.

Henderson, Hazel. *Building a Win-Win World: Life Beyond Global Economic Warfare.* Berrett-Koehler, 1996.

Hildebrand, Carol. "Making KM Pay Off." *CIO Enterprise Magazine,* Feb 15, 1999.

Holtshouse, Dan. "The Knowledge Advantage." presentation for *OD Network Annual Conference,* October 2000.

Janoff, Sandra, and Marvin Ross Weisbord. *Future Search*. Berrett-Koehler, 2000.

Jaworski, Joe, and C Otto Sharmer. "Leading in the Digital Economy: Sensing and Seizing Emerging Opportunities." *Dialog on Leadership,* December 2000.

Kaplan, Robert, and David P Norton. *The Balanced Scorecard.* Harvard Business School Press, 1996.

Kaplan, Robert, and David P Norton. *The Strategy-Focused Organizations: How Balanced Scorecard Companies Thrive in the New Business Environment.* Harvard Business School Press, 2001.

Kauffman, Stuart. *At Home in the Universe: The Search for Laws of Self-Organization and Complexity.* Oxford University Press, 1995.

Kelly, Kevin. *New Rules for the New Economy: Ten Radical Strategies for a Connected World.* Viking Press, 1998.

Kirkpatrick, David. "Great Leap Forward: From Davos, Talk of Death." *Fortune,* March 5, 2001.

Krebs, Valdis. "Managing Core Competencies of the Corporation." *The Advisory Board Company,* 1996. Available at www.orgnet.com.

Kuhn, Thomas S. *The Structure of Scientific Revolutions, 2nd Edition.* University of Chicago Press, 1970.

Kuichi, Tachi and Bill Shireman. *What we Learned in the Rainforest: Business Lessons From Nature.* Berrett-Koehler, 2002.

Lave, Jean, and Etienne Wenger. *Situated Learning: Legitimate Peripheral Participation.* Cambridge University Press, 1991.

Lesser, Eric and John Storch. "Communities of Practice and Organizational Performance." *IBM Systems Journal,* Vol 40, No 4, 2001.

Lev, Baruch. "Intangibles: Management, Measurement and Reporting." *Brookings Institution,* 2001. Available through www.brook.edu.

Levering, Robert, and Milton Moskowitz. "The 100 Best Companies to Work For." *Fortune,* February 4, 2000.

Levine, Rick, Christopher Locke, Doc Searles, and David Weinberger. *The Cluetrain Manifesto: The end of business as usual.* Perseus Books, 2000. Also see www.cluetrain.com.

Lietaer, Bernard. *The Future of Money: Creating New Wealth, Work and a Wiser World.* London: Century, 2001.

Linder, Jane, Alvin Jacobsen, Matthew D Breitfelder, and Mark Arnold, "Business Transformation Outsourcing: Partnering for Radical Change." Accenture Institute for Strategic Change, July 18, 2001.

Longworth, David. "Finding E-Content Contentment." *Destination CRM.com.* December 4, 2001.

March, James G. *The Pursuit of Organizational Intelligence.* (Introduction), Blackwell Business Press, 1999.

Maturana, Humberto R and Francisco J Varela. *The Tree of Knowledge: The Biological Roots of Human Understanding.* Shambala, 1987.

McDermott, Richard and Vic Gulas. "Knowledge Communities at Montgomery Watson Harza." Presentation for *Braintrust,* San Francisco, February 2002.

Neef, Dale. *A Little Knowledge Is a Dangerous Thing: Understanding Our Global Knowledge Economy.* Butterworth-Heinemann, 1999.

Nonaka, Ikujiro, and Hirotaka Takeuchi. *The Knowledge Creating Company: How Japanese Companies Create the Dynamics of Innovation.* Oxford University Press, 1995.

Orr, Julian. *Talking About Machines: An Ethnography of a Modern Job.* IRL Press, 1996.

Osterland, Andrew. "Decoding Intangibles." *CFO Magazine,* April 2001.

Owen, Harrison. *Expanding our Now: The Story of Open Space Technology.* Berrett-Koehler, 1997.

Peppers, Don, and Martha Rogers PhD. *Enterprise One to One: Tools for Competing in the Interactive Age.* Currency Doubleday, 1997.

Pfeffer, Jeffrey, and Robert I Sutton. *The Knowing-Doing Gap: How Smart Companies Turn Knowledge into Action*. Boston: Harvard Business School Press, 2000.

Polanyi, Michael. *Personal Knowledge: Towards a Post-Critical Philosophy*. Chicago University Press, 1958, 1962.

Prusak, Larry and Tom Davenport. *Working Knowledge*. Harvard Business School Press, 1998.

Ray, Paul H, and Sherry Ruth Anderson PhD. *The Cultural Creatives: How 50 Million People are Changing the World*. Harmony Books, 2000.

Reuthe, Elizabeth, and Verna Allee. "Knowledge Management: Moving the Case Model from a Snapshot to a Story." *Health Forum Journal*, May/June 1999.

Ruggles, Rudy, and Dan Holtshouse, Editors. *The Knowledge Advantage: 14 Visionaries Define Marketplace Success in the New Economy*. Capstone, 1999.

Rumizen, Melissie. *The Complete Idiot's Guide to Knowledge Management*. Alpha, 2001.

Sahtouris, Elisabet. "Living Systems: The Internet and Human Future." presentation, *Planetwork*, Global Ecology and Information Technology, San Francisco, May 2000. Available at www.sahtouris.com.

Schwerin, David A, PhD. *Conscious Capitalism: Principles for Prosperity*. Butterworth-Heinemann, 1998.

Senge, Peter. *The Fifth Discipline: The Art and Practice of the Learning Organization*. Currency/Doubleday, 1990.

Shapiro, Carl, and Hal R Varian. *Information Rules: A Strategic Guide to the Network Economy*. Boston: Harvard Business School Press, 1999.

Shell Oil. *People, Planet & Profits: The Shell Report*. Summary 2001.

Snowden, Dave. "The Art and Science of Story or "Are You Sitting Uncomfortably?'." *Business Information Review*, December, 2000.

Stemke, Jeff. "Using Best Practice Teams and Communities of Practice to Accelerate Innovation Deployment." Presentation at *Braintrust*, Scottsdale, AZ, February, 2000.

Stewart, Thomas A. *The Wealth of Knowledge: Intellectual Capital and the Twenty-First Century Organization.* Currency Doubleday, 2001.

Sullivan, Gordon R, and Michael V Harper. *Hope Is Not a Method: What Business Leaders Can Learn from America's Army.* Random House, 1996.

Sveiby, Karl-Erik. *The New Organizational Wealth: Managing and Measuring Knowledge-Based Assets.* San Francisco: Berrett-Koehler, 1997.

Szulanski, Gabriel, and Sidney Winter. "Getting it Right the Second Time." *Harvard Business Review*, January 2002.

Szulanski, Gabriel. *Inter-Firm Transfer of best Practices Project.* American Productivity and Quality Center, Houston, Texas, 1994.

Szulanski, Gabriel and James Lovelock. *Earthdance: Living Systems in Evolution.* Universe.com, 2000.

Tapscott, Don, David Ticoll, and Alex Lowy. *Digital Capital: Harnessing the Power of Business Webs.* Harvard Business School Press, 2000.

U.S. Census Bureau statistics. *Employment Size of Firms.* 1999.

U.S. Small Business Administration. *Small Business Economic Indicators* 2000. Office of Advocacy, 2001.

Wasserman, Stanley, and Katherine Faust. *Social Network Analysis: Methods and Applications.* Cambridge University Press, 1994.

Webster's Universal Encyclopedic Dictionary. Barnes & Noble Books, 2002.

Wenger, Etienne. "Communities of Practice: Stewarding Knowledge." November, 1999. Article available through the author at www.wenger.com.

Wenger, Etienne, Richard McDermott, and William M Snyder. *Cultivating Communities of Practice: A Guide to Managing Knowledge.* Harvard Business School Press, 2002.

Wenger, Etienne. *Communities of Practice: Learning, Meaning and Identity.* Cambridge University Press, 1998.

Wheatley, Margaret J and Myron Kellner-Rogers. *A Simpler Way.* Berrett-Koehler, 1996.

Wheatley, Margaret J. *Leadership and the New Science: Learning about Organization from an Orderly Universe.* Berrett-Koehler, 1992.

Wheatley, Margaret J. *Turning to One Another: Simple Conversations to Restore Hope to the Future.* Berrett-Koehler, 2002.

Wiig, Karl. "What Future Knowledge Management Users May Expect." *Journal of Knowledge Management,* Vol 3, No 2, 1999, p 157.

Wilber, Ken. *The Atman Project.* Wheaton, Ill: Theosophical Publishing, 1980.

About the Author

Verna Allee, M.A. is an internationally recognized thought leader in knowledge management, intangibles and new business models. In July 2001, KM Magazine named her one of the top six movers and shakers in the knowledge management field. Through her *Verna Allee Associates* value network she consults in strategic issues and knowledge management with Motorola, Eli Lilly, Hewlett Packard (now HP), Department of the Environment Canada, MWH Global Inc. Sun Microsystems, PeopleSoft, Chubb & Son, Samtel, American Express India, Unocal, Assurant Group, Oracle, Seagate Technologies, Rockwell Avionics, Unisys, Clarica, AT&T, Chevron, Steelcase, innovative start ups and purposeful networks.

Verna is a frequent keynote speaker at conferences nationally and abroad and is a Fellow of the World Business Academy. She acts as advisor for special projects in intellectual capital and the knowledge economy with Stanford University, the Brookings Institution and Digital4Sight. She is an adjunct faculty member of Alliant International University, holds degrees in Social Science and The Study of Human Consciousness from U.C. Berkeley and JFK University and guest lectures at universities around the world.

Her publications include her groundbreaking book, *The Knowledge Evolution: Expanding Organizational Intelligence,* 1997. She is also a contributor to a variety of business journals, books and prestigious reports. Her forthcoming publications include *What Is True Wealth and How Do We Create It?,* co-edited with Dinesh Chandra (Sharma Publishers, India). Through partner Know Inc Verna has also published the *Verna Allee Toolkit*™, supporting the *HoloMapping*™ and *ValueNet Works*™ methods with web-enabled learning modules and applications, (http://www.alleetoolkit.com.)

Index